Welcome Back, Jesus!

Welcome Back, Jesus!

W. A. Criswell

Broadman Press
Nashville, Tennessee

Subject heading: JESUS CHRIST—SECOND COMING
Dewey Decimal Classification: 232.6
Library of Congress Catalog Card Number: 76-27482
Printed in the United States of America

Dedication

To that faithful remnant, the invisible
church within the visible church, who is
watching, waiting, praying, for the soon
return of our Lord . . . ready to welcome
him back to earth in the same manner "as
he went away" (Acts 1:11).

Foreword

There is a little book I have written entitled *Joining the Church.* It is taught to all the children in our congregation before they are received for baptism and church membership. After passing the test on the little book, the children are brought to me by their parents, and I then ask the child certain questions about the chapters they have studied. For this pastoral discussion I will always say to the youngster, "Jesus closed the ordinance of the Lord's Supper with this sentence: 'For as often as ye eat this bread, and drink this cup, ye do shew the Lord's death till he come.' " Then I faithfully ask, "What does the Lord mean by those words, 'Till he come?' " Without exception the child will always answer, "That means Jesus is coming again." I then ask, "Do you believe you will see Jesus some day?" The reply never fails, "Yes, when he comes to take us up to heaven." I then avow, "I believe that, too; Paul calls this promise of the Lord's return 'the blessed hope.' "

It has been a precious experience for me to write this volume for Broadman Press entitled, WELCOME BACK, JESUS! after their publishing the previous volume entitled *What to Do Until Jesus Comes Back.* Earnestly do I pray that the dear Savior will no less bless and encourage you who read the words as he blessed me in writing them.

My deepest gratitude is herein expressed to those who helped prepare the manuscript for publication. Most especially do I thank Zola Levitt, "a completed Jew," a faithful Christian believer in the household of Israel, for his invaluable assistance in making the chapters more readable. He is a gifted author in his own right.

Maranatha! Till he come!

W. A. CRISWELL

First Baptist Church
Dallas, Texas

Contents

1
The Witness of the New Testament to the Return of Our Lord

Is Jesus really, literally, coming again? Truly and actually? We not only have the testimony of the Old Testament prophets concerning the blessed return of our Lord but we also have the testimony of Jesus himself. We have the Lord's own faithful words of promise. And as if that were not enough, we have many, many added details in the apostolic writings and in the mighty Apocalypse. It seems as though the early church was consumed with the passion of the early and triumphant return of our Lord.

The Lord Jesus Speaks Concerning His Return

When Jesus was in the upper room in the city of Jerusalem with his eleven apostles gathered around him, he told them he was going away from them, and that he was going to return for them (John 13:33 to 14:3). This is the first time he had plainly spoken to them of his going to the Father's house, and his coming back. His disciples were very sad and troubled at the thought of his leaving them. He had guided them, taught them, and empowered them. Now, who was going to do those things for them? They were confused, and it caused them to falter in deepest perplexity. But Christ comforted his disciples with the precious promise that he would come again. He said:

"In my Father's house are many mansions: if it were not so, I would have told you. I go to prepare a place for you. And if I go and prepare a place for you, I will come again, and receive you unto myself; that where I am, there ye may be also" (John 14:2-3).

All of the details of this return are made known by the further words of Jesus and by the Spirit through the apostles. But here we have the sweet promise, the blessed hope from the lips of our dear Savior. And this same Jesus who gave us this promise gives it to us again for the last time in his own words from heaven, "Surely I come quickly" (Rev. 22:20). The one who said "I go" is the one who says "I come."

Many people say that the only "coming" of the Lord for which we are to look is a "spiritual" coming, or "a coming to the heart." There is a sense in which the Lord comes and dwells in the hearts of the believers (Eph. 3:17), but this is not the fulfillment of the promise of the Lord, "I will come again and receive you unto myself." Nothing but his personal return and presence can fulfill the promise or satisfy the heart. Jesus has carried his manhood with him unto heaven, and there he lives as the God-man. And as such he will come again. Even the angels, those heavenly beings who stood before the disciples at the ascension of Christ, avowed a like promise. They said, "This same Jesus, which is taken up from you into heaven, shall so come in like manner as ye have seen him go into heaven" (Acts 1:11).

During the days of the ministry of our Lord, he spoke so often and so plainly of the end times. The parable of the tares is so typical of his delineation concerning the end of the world. Jesus gave the interpretation in Matthew 13:37-43:

"He answered and said unto them, He that soweth the good seed is the Son of man;

The field is the world; the good seed are the children of the kingdom; but the tares are the children of the wicked one;

The enemy that sowed them is the devil; the harvest is the end of the world; and the reapers are the angels.

As therefore the tares are gathered and burned in the fire; so shall it be in the end of this world.

The Son of man shall send forth his angels, and they shall gather out of his kingdom all things that offend, and them which do iniquity;

And shall cast them into a furnace of fire: there shall be wailing and gnashing of teeth.

Then shall the righteous shine forth as the sun in the kingdom of their Father. Who hath ears to hear, let him hear."

Here Jesus plainly teaches that the tares shall continue to grow with the wheat, and that the wicked shall continue to dwell with the righteous on this earth until Christ returns. "The end of the age" refers to the second coming of Christ which is to introduce the messianic judgment. The same thing is taught in the parable of the net (Matt. 13:47-50).

In Matthew Jesus spoke of our rewards when he comes:

"For the Son of man shall come in the glory of his Father with his angels; and then he shall reward every man according to his works" (16:27).

"When the Son of man shall come in his glory, and all the holy angels with him, then shall he sit upon the throne of his glory: And before him shall be gathered all nations; and he shall separate them one from another, as a shepherd divideth his sheep from the goats" (25:31-32)·

The coming of the Son of man always refers to our Lord's second advent when he returns to set up his kingdom. This passage goes on through verse 46. It depicts a great separation of the believers and unbelievers. The sheep are those in whom divine life is manifested by their loving care for those who belong to Christ, his brethren. Both classes had done what was natural to them, for their acts were the natural outcome of their character. The sheep are the righteous. The goats are the unrighteous. The salvation of people will not be on the ground of works, but their works will prove the reality of their faith.

An apocalyptic address was delivered by our Lord, recorded in Matthew 24. He says that his return will be as lightning that shines from the east to the west. He will be illuminating the whole heaven. He will come in the *Shekinah* clouds of glory in great power accompanied by angels and saints (Jude 14, 1 Thess. 3:13). We learn from other passages of Scripture that then the throne of David will be set up again in Jerusalem, and Christ will begin his millennial reign.

In Matthew 23:27-28 the Lord Jesus stood weeping over lost Jerusalem whose house was left empty and desolate. The chapter ends in fierce judgment. Jesus departed from the Temple physically and spiritually, and he says, "Ye shall not see me henceforth, till ye shall say, Blessed is he that cometh in the name of the Lord" (v. 39). The leaders of the nation of Israel will not see him again until he returns in glory and they acknowledge him as the Messiah and receive him as the one who comes from God. God is now gathering out of all nations a people in the name of Jesus, and not until that work is completed will Israel as a nation acclaim their Lord as their Redeemer and King.

And lest we be prone to forget the mighty presence of

our promised, reigning King who is coming again, we are
ever mindful of the testimony of the Lord's Supper: "For
as often as ye eat this bread, and drink this cup, ye do
shew the Lord's death till he come" (1 Cor. 11:26). The
Lord's Supper is a memorial feast. It looks back to the
"cross" and forward to the "coming."

The Witness of the Apostles to the Return of Christ

For a moment, let us reread the inspired words of the
apostles themselves as they spoke concerning the return
of our Lord.

Paul wrote:

"For our conversation is in heaven; from whence also
we look for the Saviour, the Lord Jesus Christ:

Who shall change our vile body, that it may be fashioned
like unto his glorious body, according to the working
whereby he is able even to subdue all things unto himself"
(Phil. 3:20-21).

James, the pastor of the church at Jerusalem, wrote:

"Be patient therefore, brethren, unto the coming of the
Lord. Behold, the husbandman waiteth for the precious
fruit of the earth, and hath long patience for it, until he
receive the early and latter rain.

Be ye also patient; stablish your hearts: for the coming
of the Lord draweth nigh" (Jas. 5:7-8).

Simon Peter wrote concerning those who ridicule the
idea of a coming Lord:

"Knowing this first, that there shall come in the last
days scoffers, walking after their own lusts,

And saying, Where is the promise of his coming? for since the fathers fell asleep, all things continue as they were from the beginning of the creation" (2 Pet. 3:3-4).

"But, beloved, be not ignorant of this one thing, that one day is with the Lord as a thousand years, and a thousand years as one day.

The Lord is not slack concerning his promise, as some men count slackness; but is longsuffering to us-ward, not willing that any should perish, but that all should come to repentance.

But the day of the Lord will come as a thief in the night; in the which the heavens shall pass away with a great noise, and the elements shall melt with fervent heat, the earth also and the works that are therein shall be burned up" (2 Pet. 3:8-10).

Satan has caused many to scoff by mingling the second coming of Christ with different forms of false teaching. Satan always offers a counterfeit or a perverted doctrine, but why should evangelical Christians give us this blessed hope and sure promise of Christ's literal kingdom on earth? Some of the greatest evangelists have cherished this blessed hope—John and Charles Wesley, Charles Haddon Spurgeon, D. L. Moody, James Hudson Taylor, R. A. Torrey, Robert G. Lee, and a host of others. The word of God abounds in warning to the sinner and in comfort to the saint based on the promise of the sure return of Jesus Christ to the earth.

Peter wrote again in his second epistle, "For we have not followed cunningly devised fables, when we made known unto you the power and coming of our Lord Jesus Christ, but were eyewitnesses of his majesty" (1:16). Peter here refers to the transfiguration of Christ on the mount

(Matt. 17:1-5), which was a type of his second coming. Moses was a type of the resurrected saints, and Elijah of those who shall be translated without dying.

Jude, the brother of James who was pastor of the mother church at Jerusalem, wrote:

"And Enoch also, the seventh from Adam, prophesied of these, saying, Behold, the Lord cometh with ten thousands of his saints, To execute judgment upon all, and to convince all that are ungodly among them of all their ungodly deeds which they have ungodly committed, and of all their hard speeches which ungodly sinners have spoken against him" (Jude 14-15).

The aged apostle John said in his first epistle, "And now, little children, abide in him; that, when he shall appear, we may have confidence, and not be ashamed before him at his coming" (2:28).

John also wrote in his first letter these words: "Every man that hath this hope in him purifieth himself, even as he is pure" (3:3). This hope grips the soul and changes the life. It changes idle Christians into zealous soul-winners. The thought that at any moment the church may be caught away to be with Christ makes the child of God want to be ready for his coming. The desire to snatch people from the clutches of Satan before it is too late makes one go out into the highways and byways to win people to Christ. No truth causes a man to hold so loosely to the things of time as does this doctrine.

The Mystery of the Church and the Kingdom

The church and the church age were a secret God kept in his heart until the fullness of the times to reveal it. The kingdom was no mystery. The Old Testament prophets talk about it. But there was something that was a "mystery" to them—and that was what was to come in between the cross and the crown. Jesus said he was going to build the church, but he did not say when it should appear (Matt. 16:13-20). The "mystery of the church" was first revealed to Paul:

"For this cause I Paul, the prisoner of Jesus Christ for you Gentiles, If ye have heard of the dispensation of the grace of God which is given me to you-ward: How that by revelation he made known unto me the mystery; (as I wrote afore in few words, Whereby, when ye read, ye may understand my knowledge in the mystery of Christ) Which in other ages was not made known unto the sons of men, as it is now revealed unto his holy apostles and prophets by the Spirit; That the Gentiles should be fellow-heirs, and of the same body, and partakers of his promise in Christ by the gospel" (Eph. 3:1-6).

From this we see that the church was unknown to the Old Testament prophets. The king having been rejected, it was impossible then to set up the kingdom, so the kingdom took on another aspect known as "The Kingdom in Mystery." If we want to know about this "Kingdom in Mystery," which comes at the time between the ascension of Christ and the rapture of the church, we must study the parables in Matthew 13.

The word *church* comes from the Greek word *ekklesia* which means "assembly" or a congregation of "called-out ones." So, the church is a "called-out" body. James says in Acts 15:13-18 that God has visited the Gentiles to take out of them a people for his name. The church is that called-out body of which Christ is the Head (Eph. 1:22-23).

We are told how the body is formed in 1 Corinthians 12:12-13. The Spirit-filled, God-breathed birthday of the church was on the day of Pentecost (Acts 2:1-4). God is calling out and into his church any Jew and any Gentile who will receive Christ as Savior.

But the church age does not do away with the kingdom age. After Christ was resurrected, the hope of a visible kingdom was revived. Just before Christ ascended, his disciples asked him if he would restore the kingdom of Israel then. His reply was, "It is not for you to know the times or the seasons, which the Father hath put in his own power" (Acts 1:7). It is clear from the question of the disciples that they were looking for an earthly and visible kingdom. If Jesus had come to set up a spiritual kingdom only in this age, he would have told his disciples about it. But he did not. He confirmed their hope for an earthly kingdom, but the time had not yet come.

Let us look carefully at Luke 19:11-12:

"And as they heard these things, he added and spake a parable, because he was nigh to Jerusalem, and because they thought that the kingdom of God should immediately appear.

He said therefore, A certain nobleman went into a far country to receive for himself a kingdom, and to return."

Jesus is the "certain nobleman" who has gone into a far country (heaven) to receive a kingdom and when he has received it, he will return. So, while Jesus was born "King of the Jews," he does not become King until he actually takes the throne. At present he is in heaven with the Father, engaged in his high priestly functions, interceding for us. He is our advocate. But the day is coming with all certainty when he is coming back from heaven to set up his righteous reign on earth.

We Are Looking for That Blessed Hope, Christ Jesus Himself

Now let us see what is the next event in God's prophetic program. Some are expecting the tribulation period; some are anticipating Armageddon; some are looking for the Beast and the False Prophet. But no! The believer is looking only for the "Blessed Hope," the personal appearing of the Lord Jesus Christ. That event set before the believer, for which we are looking, is the translation or rapture of the church. When God is ready to terminate this age in which we live, the Lord Jesus Christ will appear in the air to take all believers to himself.

Oftentimes students of prophecy do not distinguish between Christ's coming *for* his saints, and *with* his saints. The former is called the *rapture* and the latter is called the *revelation.* Between the two there is a period of at least seven years during which the church is "judged" and the "Marriage of the Lamb" takes place in the heavenlies, and on the earth Antichrist manifests himself, and the tribulation runs its course. Many passages speak of Christ coming with his saints (1 Thess. 3:13; Jude 14), but it is evident that they cannot come "with" him if they had not been previously caught out "to him" (1 Thess. 4:13-17). The church is caught up before the tribulation period begins (Rev. 3:10). After Revelation 4, the church is seen no more upon the earth until she appears in Revelation 19 coming with the Bridegroom from heaven.

Jesus Christ will descend "as a thief" to the earth, coming from heaven. While he is yet in the air, the believers will be taken up to meet him in the clouds (1 Thess. 4:16-17). On the other hand, when he shall come to judge the

nations, he shall appear openly with his saints and place
his feet on the Mount of Olives (Zech. 14:4). Jesus is even
now preparing for the rapture of his people. In John 13:21
we see the announcement of Christ's approaching death.
Peter said, "Lord, whither goest thou? Jesus answered him,
Whither I go, thou canst not follow me now; but thou
shalt follow me afterwards" (John 13:36).

The disciples saw that they were going to be separated
from Jesus, and they felt that they were left as orphans.
But Jesus said, "If I go and prepare a place for you, I
will come again, and receive you unto myself; that where
I am, there ye may be also" (John 14:3). The Greek word
hetoimaso, translated here "prepare," is not the word which
means "to make" or "to manufacture." It means "to ready
up," "to furnish," "to make into a suitable habitation."
So Jesus is pictured here, not as creating a new dwelling
place, but as taking an existing habitation and preparing
and equipping it as a suitable place for those whom he
will receive to himself at his coming.

Our Lord said, "In my Father's house are many mansions." Jesus is saying that in his Father's house are many
monai, "dwelling places." This emphasizes the fact of the
unity of the family—united one with another and with the
Father. Jesus is preparing a dwelling place as a bridegroom does for his bride that we might be in his presence,
at home with him forever.

This rapture of the saints is described in 1 Thessalonians
4:14-17:

"For if we believe that Jesus died and rose again, even
so them also which sleep in Jesus will God bring with
him.

For this we say unto you by the word of the Lord, that
we which are alive and remain unto the coming of the

Lord shall not prevent them which are asleep.

For the Lord himself shall descend from heaven with a shout, with the voice of the archangel, and with the trump of God: and the dead in Christ shall rise first:

Then we which are alive and remain shall be caught up together with them in the clouds, to meet the Lord in the air: and so shall we ever be with the Lord."

Thus, we see that the rapture will be twofold:

(1) the resurrection of the "dead in Christ"

(2) the translation of the "living saints." Paul also emphasizes this twofold character of the rapture in 1 Corinthians 15:51-57:

"Behold, I shew you a mystery; We shall not all sleep, but we shall all be changed,

In a moment, in the twinkling of an eye, at the last trump: for the trumpet shall sound, and the dead shall be raised incorruptible, and we shall be changed.

For this corruptible must put on incorruption, and this mortal must put on immortality.

So when this corruptible shall have put on incorruption, and this mortal shall have put on immortality, then shall be brought to pass the saying that is written, Death is swallowed up in victory.

O death, where is thy sting? O grave, where is thy victory?

The sting of death is sin; and the strength of sin is the law.

But thanks be to God, which giveth us the victory through our Lord Jesus Christ."

The "dead in Christ" will hear the sound and will rise first. There will be no graves so deep but what the sound will reach their depths. Whether the cemeteries will be shattered by the exodus, and thus testify to the fact of the literal bodily resurrection of the dead, or whether the sainted dead will slip out of their sepulchres without disturbing them, as Christ arose and left the tomb without breaking the seal (the angel rolling away the stone simply to show that the tomb was empty), we are not told. Only the event itself will disclose the manner of the first resurrection.

We who remain until the coming of the Lord shall not precede these dead saints to glory. We shall have no advantage over them. It is as if the good hand of God holds us back for a breathtaking second. Then, in the greatest moment of eternity, this prophecy says that we shall all be glorified and instantly snatched away from the earth. Here is a picture of reunion. We shall not go to heaven apart from them, and they shall not go apart from us. The dead and the living saints shall be raptured simultaneously. We will all be called to our Lord in the clouds. We talk about flights through outer space; flights to the moon or to Jupiter; but nothing will compare with this glorious flight into heaven itself. We shall meet the Lord in the air. In a moment we shall forget every care, every heartache, every trial; all these will vanish, and all tears shall be wiped away.

After the rapture, what takes place? There are many judgments spoken of in Scripture, but there are two outstanding ones. The first is the *judgment seat of Christ.* This has to do with believers, and occurs after the rapture. The second is *the judgment of the great white throne.* This is concerned with the unbelievers and occurs after the millenium (Rev. 20:11-15).

What is the reason for the judgment seat of Christ that will take place after the rapture? Is it to determine whether one is lost or saved? No! That is determined on this earth

when we accept Christ as our Savior. Then is it to punish
the believer for his sins? No! The sins of all believers have
been judged on the cross (2 Cor. 5:21; Heb. 10:17). Then,
what is it for? The judgment seat of Christ is a judgment
of the believer's works (1 Cor. 3:11-15). The life, the walk,
and the works of the Christian must be reviewed by the
Lord, and rewarded accordingly (2 Cor. 5:10; Rom. 14:10).
At the great white throne, the unbelievers will be
judged because of their sinful works.

What will happen after the judgment of the believer's
works? It will be "the marriage of the Lamb" (Rev. 19:7-8).
The bride (the church) will be presented to the Groom
(Christ) at the rapture (2 Cor. 11:2). After the judgment
seat of Christ, the bride will return with her Groom back
to this earth. She will be clothed in fine linen, which is
the righteous acts of the saints. The Greek word is not
"righteousness" but "righteousnesses" or "righteous acts"
(Rev. 19:8). The word *dikaiomata* includes all the results
of service produced by the Holy Spirit. The church does
not put on her wedding garment until after she has been
tried at the judgment seat, where all her false works (services not done for the glory of Christ) will be consumed
by fire (1 Cor. 3:11-15).

When Christ returns to earth, he will come to the Mount
of Olives (Zech. 14:4), the point of his departure on the
occasion of his ascension into heaven recorded in Acts
1. The second coming begins with fearful manifestations
(Luke 21:25-26). Then in the midst of this, the heavens
open and Jesus comes forth!

An Appeal That We Accept Christ Jesus
as Our Savior

God has, because of his infinite mercy, delayed the
execution of his wrath on this rebellious world. It is not

necessary for anyone to perish in that dreadful, final judgment, because God has provided a remedy (John 3:16).
And he is not willing that any should perish (2 Peter 3:9).

Remember, at that day the door of mercy will be closed,
and the day of grace will be ever:

"And to you who are troubled rest with us, when the
Lord Jesus shall be revealed from heaven with his mighty
angels,

In flaming fire taking vengeance on them that know
not God, and that obey not the gospel of our Lord Jesus
Christ:

Who shall be punished with everlasting destruction from
the presence of the Lord, and from the glory of his power;

When he shall come to be glorified in his saints, and
to be admired in all them that believe (because our testimony among you was believed) in that day" (2 Thess.
1:7-10).

This invasion of Christ to earth will be in the midst
of the campaign of Armageddon, which is a holocaust that
will break out upon the earth to give this world the greatest
bloodbath it has ever seen (Rev. 14:19-20). The armies
of the whole world will be engaged in this campaign which
will cover the whole of Palestine. To read of this campaign
we turn to Revelation 19, where we see the return of our
Lord Jesus Christ in the midst of that fearful war.

The stage is so set for these events to unfold any time
God gives the signal, and takes the Restrainer (the Holy
Spirit) and the Christians up to heaven. If you do not know
Jesus as your Savior, should these events unfold, you would
have to see him as the Judge and not as the King, and
he would have to say to you, "Depart from me, ye cursed,
into everlasting fire, prepared for the devil and his angels"

(Matt. 25:41). But God offers you a Savior, who is sufficient and who can remove every sin and translate you into his presence while God pours out his wrath upon the earth.

So, Jesus Christ is coming back to earth a second time (Rev. 19:11-20). He is coming that he might reign as "KING OF KINGS, AND LORD OF LORDS" and might manifest his sovereign authority upon this earth. Before him "every knee should bow, . . . and that every tongue should confess that Jesus Christ is Lord" (Phil. 2:10-11). So it is good to look beyond the cross, beyond the empty tomb, beyond his present intercession, and look at that day when he shall come to this earth to manifest his glory. He owns the earth because he is the Creator and the Redeemer. The title deed to the earth belongs to him (Rev. 5).

Jesus Christ must come back to earth to complete his work. Not that there is anything to add to the expiation of sins effected at Calvary, for there all was accomplished! But all the plans of God are not yet realized. Hebrews 2:8-9 says, "We see not yet all things put under him." After the ascension, the Lord in his grace left this earth for this long period of time during which we could accept the gospel. But when the time of God's patience shall have elapsed, Jesus Christ will appear to complete his work in the following three domains:

(1) To deliver his own
(2) To judge the sinful world
(3) To establish his eternal reign of justice and peace.

The person who receives Christ as Savior has eternal life (John 5:24; 1 John 5:13), but we are not yet in possession of complete salvation. Our sorrows continue, and our failures, too, while the enemy wages a merciless war against us. But let us take courage. Soon we shall burst into song, for Jesus is coming to take us home.

"And not only they, but ourselves also, which have the firstfruits of the Spirit, even we ourselves groan within ourselves, waiting for the adoption, to wit, the redemption of our body.

For we are saved by hope: but hope that is seen is not hope: for what a man seeth, why doth he yet hope for?" (Rom. 8:23-24).

What we are able to experience here on earth now represents the earnest of eternal salvation (Eph. 1:13-14). But who is satisfied with the pledge? We want Jesus' promised fullness. That will be when he takes us up at the rapture and then brings us down to earth with him to reign with him. The armies that are with him at his second advent will all be believers (Rev. 19:14). The King himself is absent now, and his will is not done on earth as in heaven. The world in revolt sinks in mire and blood. The promises of Scripture are not yet all fulfilled. That is why Jesus shall return in his glory and cause peace and justice to reign on earth for a thousand years. But the earthly kingdom, as glorious as it may be, cannot last forever. Mankind of the millennium will certainly be happy and submit to the King of kings, but there will still be found in its midst men who attempt to revolt one last time against the Lord (Rev. 20:7-9). It is then that God will make all things new, and he will transport all his own to the heavenly Jerusalem, where there will be no more death, nor crying, nor sorrow, nor sin (Rev. 21:1-5). This kingdom will last forever.

In Revelation 19:1-6 we see the heavenly choir singing, "Praise our God." They rejoice at Christ's coming to take his rightful reign over the earth. He purchased the title deed to the earth at the cross, but he has not yet exercised

his right to the rulership of this earth. He will do that
when he comes back. "And I heard as it were the voice
of a great multitude, and as the voice of many waters,
and as the voice of mighty thunderings, saying Alleluia:
for the Lord omnipotent reigneth" (v. 6). All believers now
can rejoice with them and say, "Hallelujah, he is about
to reign." We approach the throne in humility and adoration and join the heavenly voices in singing, "The kingdoms of this world are become the kingdoms of our Lord,
and of his Christ; and he shall reign forever and ever"
(Rev. 11:15).

Jesus is surely coming again!

2
The Two Comings

Few passages in either testament sing so magnificently of the Messiah as does Isaiah 9:6-7:

"For unto us a child is born, unto us a son is given: and the government shall be upon his shoulder: and his name shall be called Wonderful, Counsellor, The mighty God, The everlasting Father, The Prince of Peace. Of the increase of his government and peace there shall be no end, upon the throne of David, and upon his kingdom, to order it, and to establish it with judgment and with justice from henceforth even for ever. The zeal of the Lord of hosts will perform this."

Like Isaiah, we tend to blend the two comings of our Lord into the world. We merge both the first and second coming. It is so easy for us to shift from one to the other. An illustration of this is given in a very beautiful and famous poem by Cecil F. Alexander, entitled "Once in Royal David's City." Consider how the poet speaks of the first and second coming directly together, following one another in the poem without a pause between.

> Once in royal David's city
> stood a lowly cattle shed
> Where a mother laid her baby

in a manger for His bed.
Mary was that mother mild,
Christ Jesus was her little child.
He came down to earth from heaven,
Who is God and Lord of all.
And His shelter was a stable
and His cradle was a stall.
With the poor and mean and lowly
lived on earth our Saviour Holy.
And our eyes at last shall see Him
through His own redeeming love,
For the child so dear and gentle
is our Lord in Heaven above.
And He leads His children on
to the place where He is gone.
Not in that poor lowly stable
with the oxen standing by.
We shall see Him, but in heaven
set at God's right hand on high,
When like stars, His children crowned
all in white shall gather round.

There is no feeling of incongruity when the poet speaks of the two comings virtually in the same breath. And this is exactly what we find in the Old Testament prophecies. The two comings are oftentimes mentioned in the same sentence. All through the pages of the Old Covenant the first and second coming of Christ appear as one great entity, one marvelous promise, one gloriously revealed truth.

It is rather like looking at a star. To our naked eyes, as we look up into the chalice of the sky, it shines as one glorious luminary orb. But if we get a telescope in some instances we will find that one star is not one; it is two. And they are separated, one behind the other, by millions of light years. It is like looking at a mountain range, and what appears to us as one mountain may, when we get there, be two—one behind the other with a great valley in between. So it is in the prophecies of the coming of our Lord in the Old Testament. To the prophet it looks as though the Messiah comes once. In the same breath and in the same sentence, and sometimes with the same syllable, they will speak of the coming as one, though actually it is two.

The Two Comings in the Old Testament

Early in the Old Testament, in the opening pages, we find the "protoevangelium" blending the two comings. In this "gospel before the gospel," the Lord said to the serpent, "I will put enmity between thee and the woman, and between thy seed and her seed; it shall bruise thy head, and thou shalt bruise his heel" (Gen. 3:15). In the same breath are both comings of our Lord. This is the first coming—"thou shalt bruise his heel"—you are going to nail him to a cross. But he "shall crush thy head"—that is the second coming. And yet both of them are presented there in the same breath, in the same sentence.

Now consider Genesis 49:10. Jacob, Israel, who is the prophet in this instance, turns to his fourth son, Judah, and says to him, "The sceptre shall not depart from Judah, nor a lawgiver from between his feet, until Shiloh come; and unto him shall the gathering of the people be." There are both comings in one breath. Judah will be a kingdom, he will be a nation, he will be a tribe, he will be a government until Shiloh comes. That's the first coming of our Lord. And here is the second coming—"and unto him shall the gathering of the people be." Clearly, that must refer to the second coming for there is certainly no gathering of Israel's people to Jesus now. They remain in the diaspora, scattered to the ends of the earth. But there is coming a time when Judah and the people in Israel will gather around their true Messiah, the Christ. Both comings are prophesied in the same breath.

Looking further in the Old Testament, we see Nathan the prophet speaking to King David in 2 Samuel 7:12: "And when thy days be fulfilled, and thou shalt sleep with thy fathers, I will set up thy seed after thee, [that is the first coming; and now we read the second] . . . and I will establish his kingdom." Obviously, we do not see the throne of David now on this earth, nor do we see his kingdom. But there is coming a millennial reign of our Lord when he dispenses judgment and justice to the ends of the earth on the throne of his father David. That is his second coming, yet both of them are here spoken of in the same breath.

And once again, Isaiah 9:6: "For unto us a child is born, unto us a son is given." That is the first coming. Now the second coming: "And the government shall be upon his shoulder. . . . Of the increase of his government and peace there shall be no end, upon the throne of David, and upon his kingdom, to order it, and to establish it with judgment and with justice from henceforth even for ever." That is the second coming, and they are right there side by side.

Turn just one page and here is the same juxtaposition of the two comings in Isaiah 11. "And there shall come forth a rod out of the stem of Jesse, and a Branch shall grow out of his roots: and the spirit of the Lord shall rest upon him" (vv. 1-2). That is the first coming. Now the second coming. "The wolf also shall dwell with the lamb, and the leopard shall lie down with the kid; . . . and the lion shall eat straw like the ox. . . . They shall not hurt nor destroy in all my holy mountain: for the earth shall be full of the knowledge of the Lord, as the waters cover the sea" (vv. 6-7,9). That *must* refer to the second coming because we certainly do not see that now. If the lamb dwells with the wolf now, he is on the inside of the wolf. Isaiah says that men shall not hurt nor destroy in all God's creation. But what we see in our present day is the stacking up of atomic bombs and superweapons and the improving of our disastrous potential for annihilating the human race, preparing for the final confrontation. Yet the two prophecies stand together in the same breath. "There shall come forth a rod out of the stem of Jesse, and a Branch shall grow out of his roots." The thing is cut down, but it grows back, and that is Jesus in his first coming. Then the final millennial reign is described which is the second coming.

Turn to the definitive chapter, Isaiah 53. The prophet says, "I'm going to tell you something so marvelous you simply won't believe it" ("Who hath believed our report?"). Isaiah relates, "He shall grow up before him as a tender plant, and as a root out of a dry ground: He hath no form nor comeliness; and when we shall see him there is no beauty that we should desire him. He is despised and rejected of men; a man of sorrows, and acquainted with grief; and we hid as it were our faces from him; he was despised, and we esteemed him not. Surely he hath borne our griefs, and carried our sorrows" (vv. 1-4). That is the first coming. Now look at the second coming in chapter 52. "Awake, awake; put on thy strength, O Zion; put on thy beautiful garments, O Jerusalem, the holy city: for henceforth there shall no more come into thee the uncircumcised and the unclean. Shake thyself from the dust; arise, and sit down, O Jerusalem: loose thyself from the bands of thy neck, O captive daughter of Zion" (vv. 1-2). That is the second coming. Both of them right there in the same context.

We could go on and on throughout the Old Testament. Looking at Zechariah 9:9: "Rejoice greatly, O daughter of Zion; shout, O daughter of Jerusalem: behold, thy King cometh unto thee: he is just, and having salvation; lowly,

and riding upon an ass, and upon a colt the foal of an
ass." That is the first coming. "And his dominion shall
be from sea even to sea, and from the river even to the
ends of the earth" (v. 10). That is the second coming.

Another, Malachi 3. "Behold, I will send my messenger,
and he shall prepare the way before me." That is John
the Baptist at the first coming. "And the Lord, whom ye
seek, shall suddenly come to his temple" (v. 1). That is
still the first coming. Now the second coming: "But who
may abide the day of his coming? and who shall stand
when he appeareth? for he is like a refiner's fire, and like
fullers' sope: and he shall sit as a refiner and purifier of
silver, and he shall purify the sons of Levi, and purge
them as gold and silver, that they may offer unto the Lord
an offering in righteousness" (vv. 2-3). That is the second
coming.

Clearly, the view from the Old Testament blended together the two comings of the King.

The New Testament Dilemma

Now obviously the New Testament personalities faced
quite a dilemma. If the two comings were inevitably pictured side by side in the Old Covenant, and the prophets
never saw the distance between them, how could, say, John
the Baptist reconcile those two very different comings
happening at the same time? How could Christ come lowly
and meek and despised, a man of sorrows and acquainted
with grief; and at the same time come as the Lord God
sitting on the throne of David and presiding over a dominion forever? That was a problem for the people in the
New Testament. We will see that again and again.

Consider Matthew 11: "Now when John had heard in
his prison the works of Christ, he sent two of his disciples;
and said unto him, Art thou he that should come, or do

we look for another?" (vv. 2-3). Was John suffering in
this dilemma?

Now in the commentaries and in the Sunday School
literature and in the teachings of many a Sunday School
teacher we hear, "I've read all the literature and all the
commentaries and I have prepared the lesson. This is John
the Baptist in prison. Because he is incarcerated, he is
beginning to waver and to doubt. He has lost his faith
in the Messiah, so he is trying to find out whether Jesus
is the true Messiah or not. John is overwhelmed with
doubt." That is the sort of interpretation you read univer-
sally. But the Lord himself said in the same chapter of
Matthew just a few verses down, "What do you think that
man John the Baptist is like? Is he like a reed blown in
the wind? Is he soft and effeminate like a man dressed
in the clothing of those who are filled with wine in the
king's palace? No," said Jesus. "John the Baptist is made
out of solid iron." Yet these commentators say John has
melted down because he is in prison. He is supposed to
have lost his resolve and his faith. But Jesus says just the
opposite. We must read carefully; these are the words of
the Holy Spirit. If John were doubting the Lord, Jesus
would have been the last one in the world he would have
asked about it. If John had lost his faith in Christ, he
would not ask him the question. But John the Baptist sent
to the Lord Christ and said to him, "I do not understand,
Are you that ultimate and final coming one? Or is there
yet another Christ who is coming? Are there two of them
instead of one?" That is what John wanted to know.

Make no mistake about it, John the Baptist was a man
made of blue steel. But the matter with him was the very
matter that confronted all of those who looked upon Christ
as the fulfillment of the Old Testament prophecies. They
were in a quandary. How is it that he comes to be meek

and lowly and a Savior, and at the same time he is to
be the Lord God over all the earth?

You see, John preached both comings. John preached
the first coming of the Lord when he said, "Look, there
is the Lamb of God that takes away the sin of the world.
There is the meek and lowly, suffering Lamb brought to
the slaughter, who is to carry our sins away." That is the
first coming. But John the Baptist also preached a second
coming. He stood there and said to those Pharisees and
Sadducees and all of the rest of those rulers and elders
and scribes: "The ax is laid unto the root of the trees:
therefore every tree which bringeth not forth good fruit
is hewn down and cast into the fire" (Matt. 3:10). John
the Baptist looked at them again and he said, "His win-
nowing fan is in his hand, and he is going to separate
the wheat from the chaff. The wheat is going to be gathered
into his barn. The chaff is going to be burned with un-
quenchable fire." That is the second coming of the
Lord. He is not doing that now, but he will when he
comes back again. John the Baptist preached both
comings.

Simon Peter wrestled with the same dilemma. In
Matthew 16, the Lord said, "Simon, you are a *petros* (a
firm rock), and on this *petra* (on this great confession of
faith that I am the Christ, the Son of God) I am going
to build my church." Then when the Lord announced that
he was going to be crucified and going to die, Simon Peter
said, "Be it far from thee, Lord: this shall not be unto
thee" (v. 22). The Lord turned to Simon Peter and said,
"Get thee behind me, Satan." Satan was deluding Peter.
"Get thee behind me, Satan: . . . for thou savourest not
the things that be of God, but of men" (v. 23). You see,
Simon Peter could not understand how he could die. He
could not separate the first coming from the second.

And it was not only the disciples who were confused. The common people as well had difficulty discriminating between the comings. In John 12, when the Greeks came to see him and reminded the Lord of his great kingdom made up of people from all nations who hear the gospel through the church, he said, "And I, if I be lifted up from the earth, will draw all men unto me. This he said, signifying what death he should die. The people answered him, We have heard out of the law that Christ abideth for ever: and how sayest thou, The Son of man must be lifted up?" (vv. 32-34). They did not understand. They simply did not understand the distinction of the two comings.

Looking at the disciples at the moment of Christ's ascension, we see the quandary again. In Acts 1 the disciples are watching Jesus ascend into heaven, but before he left the disciples had come to him and said, "Wilt thou at this time restore again the kingdom to Israel?" (v. 6). There is that same quandary. Where is the kingdom and where is the King? And what of its establishment in the earth? We do not understand, and here you are going back to heaven and leaving us on the earth and there is no kingdom, there is no throne of David. We do not understand.

Paul's Explanation

We finally get an explanation by the apostle Paul in Ephesians 3. Ephesians 3 is all about the resolution of the quandary of the two comings. The apostle Paul says that there is a great *musterion*. We translate it *mystery*. It is a Greek word we have taken and put in the English language, but we have changed the meaning of it. A mystery to us is a riddle hidden in an enigma, wrapped up in the inexplicable. But there is nothing of that meaning in the original Greek word. A *musterion* is a secret hidden in the heart of God; something that God kept to himself and never revealed it until he revealed it unto his apostles. There was a great *musterion*, a great secret in the heart of God that he never revealed to the prophets. But especially to Paul did Christ reveal it.

The secret was that between the first coming and the second coming, there is a day of grace. It is the day of the Holy Spirit. It is the day of the preaching of the gospel of the Son of God to both Jew and Gentile alike. It is the day of the creation of a new body, the church of Jesus Christ. The revelation given to Paul was that the Gentiles should be fellowheirs and of the same faith and of the same household and partakers of the same blessings as the chosen family of God. God never revealed that to the prophets. They simply never saw it.

When some Bible analyst takes the Old Testament and finds prophecies concerning the church he is eisegeting—reading into it something that is not literally there. So the Scriptures themselves attest to the fact that the prophets never saw the church age. They never saw this day when Gentiles can become fellowheirs of the messianic promises (Eph. 3:6). It was a *musterion* that was kept secret in the heart of God until the time that he revealed it to his holy apostles.

What God actually did was to send his Son for the first coming to be born lowly, humble, in a cattle stall. And because his parents were poor, they never had any little dresses for the baby, so they wrapped him in rags. You have it in the Bible as "swaddling clothes." They wrapped him in rags and put him on the hay. He was so poor. And he grew up like a root out of a dry ground. Who would have ever thought that out of Nazareth and out of Galilee and out of a carpenter's shop should come the Savior of the world? And he was full of grief and sorrow for the hurt of humanity. He carried our sicknesses and he shared all of our illnesses, and he died for our sins. That is the first coming. But the story is not done. The same glorious Scriptures that promise in detail the features and the outline of the coming of the Lord the first time, outline in detail the glorious coming of our Lord the second time.

The Certainty of God's Promises

If God was faithful in bringing his Son into the world the first time according to the prophets, he will be faithful also in keeping those promises when Christ comes into the world the second time. Consider how long a time passed before the prophecy of the first coming was fulfilled.

When were Adam and Eve created? Some translations of the Bible have Bishop Ussher's dates printed at the top of the page in Genesis 1. Bishop Ussher was a man of God, a noted Anglican scholar, but his calculation of dates was achieved by adding up the years listed in the genealogies throughout the Scriptures. The error here is that there were many generations, as far as we know, that were left out because the Bible was not particularly interested in naming every personality who ever existed. The Scriptures instead simply follow a line of promise. A good instance of that is found in Matthew 1:1: "Jesus Christ, the son of David, the son of Abraham."

The fact is we do not know when Adam was created. Maybe it was uncounted thousands of years ago. We do not know for sure. It is immaterial. The point is that in the day that Adam and Eve fell, in that long-ago day, God promised that there should be born of a woman him who would crush Satan's head, who would deliver us from the power of the serpent.

Now consider how long that was in the fulfilling. Recently I preached on Galatians 4:4: "When the fulness of the time was come, God sent forth his Son, made of a woman." All of the ages of history conspired to prepare for the coming of the Savior into the world. And it took centuries and millenia and still more centuries and millenia. It took thousands of years, but finally he came just exactly as the prophets had said in the Bible.

Now my brothers and sisters in Jesus, the same Lord God has promised that he is coming again. I can see the first coming. Why do I sometimes stagger before the promises of God concerning his second coming? The same Lord God that faithfully kept his word and his promises concerning the first coming will surely keep his promises and his word regarding the second coming. It will be the same blessed Jesus that we are looking for.

I do not suppose there is a liberal in the earth that believes in the return of the Lord, not a one of them. They do not believe in the virgin birth, either. They look at those promises about the coming of Jesus and they say the coming of the Lord was fulfilled in A.D. 70, in the destruction of Jerusalem; or the coming of the Lord was fulfilled in the modern advancements of science; or the coming of the Lord was fulfilled in the great humanitarian, philanthropic movements in the earth; or the coming of the Lord is fulfilled in the worldwide propagation of the gospel; or the coming of the Lord was fulfilled in the writing of the Constitution of the United States, or some other thing like that. And there are a thousand other worldly things that they mention. Is that what I am to look for? In looking for the Son of God, am I to look for the destruction of a great city, or am I to look for some advancement in science, or am I to look for some political document, or am I to look for some great international achievement? Is that what we are to look for?

What were they looking for the first time? They were

looking for the blessed Savior from heaven. What are we to look for the second time? We are to look for *that same blessed Lord from heaven.* Oh how the Lord emphasizes that in the Bible. In 1 Thessalonians 4 Paul writes, "For the Lord himself shall descend from heaven with a shout, with the voice of the archangel, and with the trump of God" (v. 16). For the Lord himself!" *The same Lord!* It is *he* who is coming. It is *he* for whom we are waiting. It is *Jesus the Christ.*

In Acts 1 those disciples are looking up into heaven, watching Jesus as he goes up into heaven. And they are just staring up into the sky. They have lost every hope, they have lost every dream. They have lost every promise. They are alone. And they stand there forlorn, watching Jesus go up into heaven. Then an angel comes and taps them on the shoulder and says, "What are you doing gazing up into heaven? This same Jesus. . . ." This *same* Jesus! It is Jesus we are looking for. We are not waiting for tribulations or woes or trumpets or destruction of cities or political instruments or achievements. We are just looking for him. "This same Jesus . . . shall so come in like manner as ye have seen him go" (v. 11). That is the second coming. And the same God that brought the promises to pass in the first, the same Lord God is going to keep his promises in the second.

> It is not for a sign we are watching,
>   for wonders above and below.
> The pouring of vials of judgment,
>   the sounding of trumpets of woe.
> It is not for a day we are looking,
>   not even a time yet to be
> When the earth shall be filled with God's glories,
>   as the waters cover the sea.
> It is not for a King we are longing
>   to make the world kingdoms His own.

It is not for a Judge who shall summon
the nations of earth to His throne.
We wait for our Lord, our beloved,
our comforter, Master and Friend.
The substance of all that we hope for,
beginning of faith in its end.
We watch for our Savior and Bridegroom
who loves us and made us His own.
For Him we are looking and longing,
for Jesus and Jesus alone.

AUTHOR UNKNOWN

He is coming! As he came the first time, in keeping
with all of the promises of God, so he will come the second
time just as God says in his book. He may delay for a
long, long time. It may be hundreds of years yet—I do
not know. God in his purpose thought it best that we should
not know. But he is coming, and it will be *the same Lord
Jesus.*

Just think what a day that will be when the heavens
are rolled back like a scroll. Accompanied by all of the
angelic hosts and the redeemed, and on clouds of the
Shekinah glory of God, he descends. Oh, can I actually
believe that these dull, stolid eyes will see that? That my
heart shall leap in expectancy of that? It is too good to
be true. The first coming was too good to be true, but
God was made flesh and dwelt among us. And he died
to carry our sins away. The second coming is too good
to be true, also.

But God said it. We believe it and are rejoicing in it.

3
The Transfiguration

Jesus uttered a startling statement of prophecy one day which has occasioned considerable commentary. This is one of those rather cryptic and far-reaching remarks of our Lord which has tended to confuse many readers of the gospel.

"Verily I say unto you, There be some standing here, which shall not taste of death, till they see the Son of man coming in his kingdom" (Matt. 16:28). No doubt his listeners were taken aback.

What did our Lord mean by that?

As we read the Bible commentaries we find many differences of opinion on this difficult Scripture. Some scholars say that Jesus means that there shall be some "standing here who shall not die until they see the glories of God in my ministry." After all, those standing by were to see marvelous things, such as the raising of Lazarus from the dead.

True, that Scripture could refer to such miracles. Certainly the magnificent glories of God were many times demonstrated in the ministry of our Lord, the Son of God.

Then there are those who suggest that Jesus means that there shall be some "standing here who shall not taste of death until they see me raised from the dead."

And surely, the Lord demonstrated in the cross and in

the resurrection his complete overcoming of the principalities and powers of darkness. He certainly burst asunder the bands of the grave and rose triumphant over the sentence of death. No doubt about that!

And that could certainly be a part of what he meant by that startling statement of prophecy.

Then there are those who suggest that this text refers to Pentecost. They tend to render it, "There be some standing here who shall not taste of death until they see the power of God poured out into this world and the glorious ministry of this age of grace is launched."

That is a good analysis, too. That Scripture could possibly refer to the power of God poured out as the Holy Spirit came at Pentecost.

Then there are those (and I am surprised at how many New Testament scholars believe this) who say that since Jesus said "some" shall not taste of death, he means that many of them will die, but *some* will be left alive. These scholars hold that the Scripture refers to a time beyond that in which most of those particular people standing by would live. They usually suggest that this particular prophecy was fulfilled in A.D. 70 when the Jewish nation was destroyed by Titus and the Roman legions. Some of those standing by, of course, were dead by that year, and some must have still been alive; and that year marked a time when the onward march of Christianity went beyond Judaism and into the Roman Empire.

There is certainly some truth in that also. There is no doubt that the Lord referred often to the coming destruction of Jerusalem in A.D. 70, such as in his great apocalyptic discourse of Matthew 24. The Lord used that holocaust as a type of the great final judgment of God at the consummation of the age. And so they conclude that the Lord avows there will be some who shall not taste of death until

A.D. 70, the beginning of the onward march of the kingdom of Jesus in the world.

Well, to wrap up all of those interpretations together, they are all fine. I have no strong objection to any of them. But there are some things about this particular text and the way it is situated in the Scriptures that gives me pause. And then there is something more that Simon Peter says in the gospel that seals a certain interpretation in my own heart.

The Scriptures Interpret the Scriptures

We seem to have a psychological inclination toward the chapter divisions of the Bible, which creates some difficulty in understanding the message. When we get to the end of a chapter, we assume that we are at the end of the discussion. And when we start another chapter, we normally think that we have started something new.

It comes as news to many people that the chapter divisions were put into the Bible some 1500 years after the text was actually written, and they are by no means inspired. They are arbitrary, selected for convenience, and they have been convenient. But there was no intention to punctuate the Scriptures in any given way when the chapter divisions were made.

The particular phrase of the Lord which we are studying now happens to appear at the end of a chapter, Matthew 16. In the seventeenth chapter, Matthew begins the story of the transfiguration of our Lord, that remarkable vision of Christ in glory observed by the startled disciples.

It is significant that Mark's gospel relates our kingdom verse just before the transfiguration narrative in Mark 9. The same arrangement of the Scriptures is apparent in Luke 9.

Looking more closely at Matthew 16 and 17, we note

that the first word of chapter 17 is "And." *And* always connects something with something else. It is a conjunction, and it puts things together. The appearance of the "and" makes me read directly from the verse about the Son of man coming in his kingdom to the narrative of the transfiguration. The chapter division, as we have seen, has no effect at separating the two passages.

Then we notice an interesting comparison if we look at the second letter which Simon Peter wrote (1:16-18). He says there that he saw the glory of Christ in the power and *parousia* of Jesus Christ. The particular choice of *parousia* in this description of the transfiguration experience is very interesting.

In the New Testament, wherever we find the word *parousia* it refers to the coming of our Lord, the second advent of Christ. Literally, it means the presence of the Lord, the coming of the Lord. Simon Peter, therefore, indicates that this story of the transfiguration of Jesus is a story of the coming of our Lord. And when the disciples looked upon the transfiguration, they saw in effect the coming of our Lord.

Now, in what sense could the transfiguration be the Lord coming in glory and power and majesty and in his kingdom? Well, I personally believe that the transfiguration is a kind of preview, a harbinger, an anticipation of how it shall be when Jesus comes again. When I read that text, I feel that I am reading a miniature, a preview of the glorious coming down of our King from heaven.

And what a glorious preview that transfiguration is! Just hear the words of this passage: "And after six days Jesus taketh Peter, James, and John his brother, and bringeth them up into an high mountain apart, and was transfigured [metamorphized] before them: and his face did shine as the sun, and his raiment was white as the light. And behold, there appeared unto them Moses and Elias talking with him. . . . While he yet spake, behold, a bright cloud overshadowed them: and behold a voice out of the cloud, which said, This is my beloved Son, in whom I am well pleased; hear ye him" (Matt. 17:1-5).

If that really is a preview, I must say I can hardly wait for the main event!

Setting the Scene

The transfiguration took place at Caesarea Philippi. The old name of the area was Dan. We are all familiar with the expression "from Dan to Beersheba." Beersheba was in the south of Israel at the lower part of the Negeb, the great desert below the Dead Sea. Dan was at the top of the holy land in the far north, at the base of Mount Hermon which is nearly 10,000 feet high and usually covered with snow. The Jordan River, which runs through a thanklessly arid country, is fed by the cool rains and the melting snows on that great Lebanese range, Mount Hermon.

That is where we find the disciples, there in the north part of Israel at Caesarea Philippi, old Dan, at the base of Mount Hermon. That is where the transfiguration took place.

The incredible moment happened about seven months before the crucifixion of Jesus. Apparently the disciples were on the mountain for an all-night prayer meeting. Luke tells the story; he says that the eyes of the disciples were heavy with sleep, and then he remarks "it came to pass, that on the next day, when they were come down . . ." (9:37). So it appears that they had spent the entire night on the mount.

The disciples, characteristic of the weariness of the flesh, fell asleep. They are our witnesses, and some might conjecture that they were reporting a dream. But actually Luke

is careful to say that the disciples observed the glory of
Christ, and they saw the two men, Moses and Elias, standing with Jesus talking to him, while they were fully awake.
This is something that happened before their normal, open
eyes. This was not a vision, a dream, or a fantasy.

There were three witnesses: Peter, James, and John. The
testimony about the event that we have appears in the
writings of Peter and John. James, the other witness, was
beheaded by Herod Agrippa I, as recorded in Acts 12.
James was martyred before he could testify, but we do
have the reports of Peter and John.

Peter wrote this: "For we have not followed cunningly
devised fables when we made known unto you the power
and [parousia] coming of our Lord Jesus Christ, but were
eyewitnesses of his majesty. For he received from God
the Father honour and glory, when there came such a voice
to him from the excellent glory, This is my beloved Son,
in whom I am well pleased. And this voice which came
from heaven we heard, when we were with him in the
holy mount" (2 Pet. 1:16-18). That is what Peter wrote
about it. John, sounding almost stupefied, writes: "And
we beheld his glory, the glory as of the only begotten of
the Father" (John 1:14).

What we can make out from these reports was that while
the disciples were there in that all-night prayer meeting,
Jesus was metamorphized. (The Greek word *morphē* means
outward shape, form, outward appearance; and *metamor-
phoō* is the verb which means a transformation, a metamorphosis. We took the Greek term directly into our language.)

So Jesus was glorified. The deity shone through his
humanity. His face was like the sun. His garments were
white as the light. There he stood in heavenly glory.

The disciples must have been stunned. They were overwhelmed! They were standing there on Mount Hermon looking upon the Lord's deity, and not only that but also upon the mortal Moses and, there on the other side of the Lord, Elias.

They saw dead men, as it were, standing with the remarkably transfigured Jesus. They must have been stunned indeed!

How did the disciples know Moses and Elias? How did they know whom they were looking at? Sometimes we hear the question posed, "Will we know each other in heaven?" Well, my predecessor at Muskogee, Dr. A. N. Hall, who pastored twenty-eight years before he died in service, gave me an interesting answer. When he heard the question, "Will we know one another in heaven?" he would say, "Friends, we will not really know one another *until* we get to heaven."

Intuitive knowledge, spiritual knowledge, knowledge like that which God bestows, without teaching, without experiencing—that is heavenly knowledge. Plainly, the disciples were living on some of that heavenly knowledge, and they knew Moses and Elias when they saw them in that luminous cloud, that burning Shekinah.

According to Simon Peter, that remarkable scene was a miniature, a preview, an earnest, a harbinger, a likeness of the *parousia*, the coming of our Lord. From what Peter said, we can fairly deduce this, and it deeply satisfies me.

When I meditate about that transfiguration, I am seeing in miniature the denouement of this age, the consummation of human history, the coming down of God in glory. It just staggers the imagination of any saint.

The Preview and the Main Event

Personally, I have looked at this little preview very carefully and very eagerly. I want to know what it will be like when the Lord comes.

Consider a moment the various parts of the scene that are described for us in the Scriptures. Look first at the burning cloud, the luminous cloud (v. 5). That burning, luminous cloud turns up often in the Scriptures. That rings a bell. We never read in the Scriptures of the presence of God where men seek him without that burning, luminous cloud always attendant, always present. Look at Revelation 1:7 which is the key text of the Apocalypse: "Behold, he cometh with *clouds;* and every eye shall see him" (author's italics).

What are those clouds? Are they mists, are they vapor? Is this a normal cloud from which rain falls? No, not at all. The word cloud hardly describes the burning, the shining that is actually the raiment of God, the garment of the Lord.

In the Old Testament that Shekinah glory is referred to as a "cloud." In the Exodus and the wilderness wandering, when the Israelites looked upon that Shekinah, they saw it as a cloud in the daytime and as a burning, consuming fire at night.

When Solomon in all his glory finished the mighty Temple of God in Jerusalem, God filled it with a cloud, his glory and presence, the Shekinah. It was so wonderful the priests could not even "stand to minister."

In Isaiah 6 the prophet saw the Lord high and lifted up and his train filled the Temple, his glory filled the earth which caused Isaiah to say that it looked to him like smoke. There again is a reference to that "cloud."

That is simply the garment of the Lord. That is what he wears. That is the glory of the Lord, the flaming Shekinah.

In the New Testament, too, when the Lord ascended to his Father, we speak of the cloud. Look at Acts 1; "a cloud received him" (v. 9). As the amazed disciples watched, Jesus was taken up from them and a cloud received him out of their sight. The Lord put on the glorious garments of God, the raiment of the Almighty, the shining Shekinah of deity. This was hardly a rain cloud, but more like the costume, if we may express it that way, of God in his glory. When he returns, we shall again see this fabulous costume, the dress, the robing, the raiment of God. "Behold he cometh with clouds and every eye shall see him."

Another thing that fascinates me in the description of our little miniature about the return of the Lord is the term *glory*. John's testimony says, "And we beheld his glory, the glory as of the only begotten of the Father" (1:14).

Now the word *glory* applied to Christ must always refer to his second coming. The first coming of our Lord, we must admit, was not in glory but in humility. He came as a servant, as a slave. He was crucified like a felon. He came despised, rejected, a man of sorrows and acquainted with grief, as Isaiah lamented. He came bowed down with the burdens of the world. He came weeping, suffering, dying. He was blasphemed; he was spat upon: his beard was plucked out; he was nailed to a heavy cross; he was buried in the earth.

Indeed, when the Lord came the first time, he hardly came in glory.

But glory will accompany the Lord in full measure when he returns. When he comes the second time, he will come in his glory. And so John said that on the mount, in that metamorphosis of our Lord, in that transfiguration, he saw the coming glory of the Lord Jesus Christ.

I do not mean to persuade, by the use of this emotional description. I think we stand on solid ground in defining the word *glory* as a reference to the second coming of Christ. There is no exception to that usage in the word of God when it is applied to Christ.

Consider Matthew 24 where Christ tells the story about the judgment of the Gentiles: "They shall see the Son of man coming in the clouds of heaven with power and great glory. And he shall send his angels with a great sound of a trumpet" (v. 30). Again, consider Mark 8:38, "Whosoever therefore shall be ashamed of me and of my words in this adulterous and sinful generation; of him also shall the Son of man be ashamed, when he cometh in the *glory* of his Father with the holy angels."

So the little preview of the return of our Lord teaches us that when we see him again, when this worn out, sinful old earth looks upon Jesus, he will be in his glory, and he will be wearing his Father's raiment. His face will look like the sun, and his garments will look like the white of the light. The Lord is coming in his glory.

Moses and Elias

Now what about Moses and Elias? What could their presence mean at this electrifying scene of the transfiguration?

Well, if this is a miniature, a preview of the coming of our Lord, then Moses represents somebody, and Elias represents somebody. I feel that the appearance of these two specific personalities out of the Old Testament Scriptures carries a deep meaning for all of us who would ponder this prophecy today.

The point is, Moses and Elias concluded their earthly ministries in different ways. Moses died, as each of us must die. But Elias was carried up to glory, translated to heaven.

And so I think that Moses represents those who have

died and who will be resurrected, immortalized, glorified, raised from the dead at the coming of our Lord. Elias, who never saw death, represents those who shall be alive when the Lord comes, who will be translated to heaven, in the twinkling of an eye, at the last trump. They shall never taste of death. Just as Elias was carried to heaven in a whirlwind, and as the horses of fire and the chariots came for the prophet, so there will be a generation who will never die. In the manner of Elias, an entire generation of Christians will be translated to glory in a moment, in the twinkling of an eye, at the last trump.

Now to look more deeply into this mystery, Moses represents those who died, who are fallen asleep in Jesus, and God will demonstrate a particularly mighty power in resurrecting that group. Obviously, it is a mighty demonstration on the part of the Lord to raise the dead bodies of all of those who fell asleep in Christ to take them to heaven.

There was some contention over the body of Moses himself if we recall the account of his death and the commentary in Jude 9. God buried Moses, but we are told that Michael the archangel disputed with Satan, contending over the body of Moses. We can wonder what the devil wanted with the dead body of Moses, and here we can enter into all kinds of speculations. Some say Satan wanted to use that body to lead Israel into idolatry, because certainly Israel revered Moses. If his body were preserved, might they not possibly make a cult of worshiping of that body?

That is possible, and it may be true. But this much we do know. The human frame, this earthly tabernacle, this body, this house in which we live, is dear and precious to God. It has a special meaning to him. And Satan seeks to destroy God's ultimate purpose for us. Naturally if God wishes to resurrect this frame, this body, so that we live again, immortalized, glorified, raised from the dead, then Satan can be counted on to try to interfere with that process.

This is the distinctive doctrine of the Christian faith: that we believe in the resurrection of the dead. God's saints, even the least of God's saints, God will raise from the dust of the ground, from the heart of the earth, from the depths of the sea. That missionary that fell on a foreign field, God saw his death and marked the place. That soldier of Jesus who was buried at sea, God marked the place. Everywhere that the body of a Christian lies, God has a special marker for the place, and God will someday raise the body of that faithful one.

Pagan philosophers and all pagan, heathen religions believe in the immortality of the soul. If you tour a museum such as in Cairo, and you see the mummies there, you cannot help but realize that they looked to immortality. They were buried wrapped up in the sheets of the book of the dead. The early American Indian was buried with his bow and arrow. In Greek philosophy, the dead one crosses the river Styx into Hades beyond. The soul of the dead one was important to pagans, and they conceived that it would be immortal.

But none of them seemed to believe in the sanctity of the body. The body was considered to be nothing. In the Roman Empire, they burned the body as if it were worthless.

That is one sure sign of a pagan, heathen philosophy. It is still true today. When the Russian cosmonaut died, they burned his body and put the ashes behind a brick in the Kremlin wall. That human body, disciplined, trained, was of no further use, in their philosophy.

But to the Christian the body is sacred. Its very structure

is sacred. The body is the house in which we shall live in heaven—this body, the very one we inhabit now. And that is why the Christians lovingly laid their dead away in the catacombs below the streets of Rome. There are miles and miles of those catacombs. The Romans burned bodies, but the Christians carefully laid them away. Some day, they knew, God would reach for those bodies and touch them. God will speak the word and those fallen, physical frames shall live again. They will be like Jesus.

It is significant for us to realize that the resurrected body of our Lord, seen by the disciples, had the scars of the nailprints in his hands. Even the scar of the spear thrust into his side was apparent. It was the same Lord Jesus, the same body, only metamorphized, raised, glorified, transfigured, and this is how it shall be with each of us.

Paul writes, significantly, "I would not have you to be ignorant, brethren, concerning them which are asleep, that ye sorrow not as others which have no hope." To the pagan, the end of the body is the end of the life. The chapter is closed, the sun is set. But we saw that Jesus died and rose again; he died and was buried and was raised from the dead. To believe that is what it is to become a Christian. That is the gospel, that is truly the good news. If we believe it, Paul says, "even so them also which sleep in Jesus [who died in the Lord] will God bring with him." Paul adds "this we say unto you by the word of the Lord." Paul is emphatically saying here that this is not a speculation on his own part, or just a hope that he holds in his own heart. He specifies that this is the word of God.

For the Lord himself has said that we who are alive and remain to the coming of the Lord "shall not prevent them which are asleep." Instead, "the Lord himself shall descend from heaven with a shout, with the voice of the archangel, and with the trump of God: and the dead in

Christ shall rise first" (1 Thess. 4:16).

"First," Paul writes. The first thing in the order of events when Jesus returns is the resurrection of the dead.

If someone approaches you and says the Messiah has come, just go to the cemetery. Those Christians who sleep there will be raised, first of all, at the coming of the Lord. *Cemetery* is a thoroughly Christian word, by the way. *Koimeterion* is Greek for sleeping place, and that is what the Christians preferred to call the place where they laid their beloved dead away. In Latin they called it *coemeterium*, a sleeping place. And when it came into our language through the French, we pronounced it cemetery. Interestingly, the world had never heard of the word until Christians used it with regard to the place where they laid their dead away. It is a sleeping place, a *koimeterion*, cemetery. And just as surely as Moses was raised from the dead and seen standing with the Lord Jesus Christ, so you will be able to see at the return of the Lord the raising of the dead from our cemeteries.

Now Elias, we said, represents those who shall be alive at the return of our Savior. They will be translated, transfigured, metamorphized, glorified.

Paul wrote, "Flesh and blood cannot inherit the kingdom of God; neither doth corruption inherit incorruption. Behold I shew you a mystery [*musterion*, a secret kept in the heart of God until he revealed it to his apostles]; We shall not all sleep." There shall be a generation of us that will never die, as Elias never died. When Jesus comes, we shall be translated, immortalized in a moment, in the twinkling of an eye, at the last trump.

What is meant by "the twinkling of an eye"? Some say it is literally the time in which our eye blinks. But frankly, the blinking of an eye is a long time compared to what this word *twinkling* means. The twinkling of an eye is actually that light of recognition when you see somebody and you recognize him.

We will surely see and recognize Jesus at the last trump. For the trumpet shall sound and the dead shall be raised incorruptible. That is first. Then all of us who remain alive shall be changed and taken in a moment, in the twinkling of an eye, in a glorious translation to heaven like that of Elias, when Jesus comes again.

This is the preview, the glorious transfiguration, of the coming of our Lord Jesus Christ.

4
When Christ Shall Appear

Colossians 3:4 is one of the rich and meaningful texts in the Bible. How beautifully written and how inspiring it is! "When Christ, who is our life, shall appear, then shall ye also appear with him in glory."

You would think for a moment that you were reading a passage written by John. It is so like John to say, "when Christ, who is our life." John writes such marvelous, cosmic phrases about the term *life:* "In him was life; and the life was the light of men" (1:4); in John 11:25, "I am the resurrection, and the life." In 1 John 1:1-2, "That . . . which our hands have handled, of the Word of life; (For the life was manifested)." John is, in a way, like Moses. They both look upon God himself. They see the excellent glory. They think where God is, and they go where God is.

Christ: Our Life

Christ is our life, and the source of all life. In John 5:24-25, there are four "verilies." "Verily, verily, I say unto you, He that heareth my word, and believeth on him that sent me, hath everlasting life, and shall not come into condemnation; but is passed from death unto life. Verily, verily, I say unto you, The hour is coming, and now is, when the dead shall hear the voice of the Son of God:

and they that hear shall live."

As God in Christ in the beginning created the heavens and the earth and the light, so Christ creates light in us. The source of light is in him.

Christ is the substance of our life, and we can read plainly enough that life is Christ and Christ is life. But what is life exactly? What is this stuff we all have as we walk upon the earth?

The medical researcher with his scalpel can probe and divide and dissect tissue and flesh, but he will never find life. The physician and the surgeon may seek and examine, may even make important repairs, but they will never discover the essence of life. Life is an elusive thing in us that no man has ever seen or touched. The brain can think about it, and the mind can grasp at it, but no man can understand the essence of life. The substance of life, the stuff of life, is God. It is Christ.

Christ is the sustenance of our life. He represents the manna from heaven, the firstfruits, the golden grain. Everything else is chaff to be blown away by the wind, but Christ is the fine, white, pure flour, the Bread of life, and the rock that followed them from which they drank. That rock from which the people in the wilderness took water was Christ, the sustenance of our life (1 Cor. 10:4).

Christ is the solace of our life. Whom have I in heaven but thee? And whom do I desire in earth if not thee? Each life on earth tends to become more solitary as time passes and family and friends are gone. But Christ remains. He is the solace of our life. Christ is the prime example of life. Jesus is the portrait, the model, the exemplar in our soul. We are to be like him; we are to have life as he is life.

There is certainly no way to express it all—"Christ who is our life." Whether we are talking about life in heaven or life on earth, the principle remains the same. The flame is the same whether it burns in the kingdom of grace or in the kingdom of glory. Christ is our life.

Christ: Life in Us

"When Christ, who is our life, shall appear, then shall ye also appear with him in glory." When he returns we will all live, whether we have previously died in the flesh or whether we remain alive.

In a sense, the life of the believer is hidden away. It is not really manifested yet. The world cannot see it, and the world cannot understand it. The life we have in us appears to be the life that every unbeliever has. But then in looking at the lowly caterpillar, it is difficult to see the life of the butterfly to come. In that sense the life, the potential *real* life, is hidden away from the world.

The worldly person, the unbeliever, listens to a preacher as he expounds the infallible word of God, and he goes away and shrugs his shoulders. "Maybe so," he thinks. He hears the sermon and like the Epicureans at Athens listening to Paul, he scoffs. Sometimes he is more courteous like the Stoics who said, "We'll hear you again concerning this matter."

The world, the unbelieving world, cannot understand, and it cannot see the hidden life of Christ in the believer. It cannot see the seed, the germinal potential of immortal life. After all, the unbelievers could not see the special life in Jesus himself, nor could they understand him when he came into the world. He was despised and rejected of men. They blasphemed and spat upon him and crucified him, and had it not been for a borrowed tomb, we can suppose that the body of Christ would have been cast away in a pauper's grave.

How different is the life hidden in the heart of the

believer from that lived by the unbeliever! Seeing Jesus, seeing him, believing in him; hearing the word of Jesus, listening to him; and finally raised with our Lord and living with him—all of this is hidden, misunderstood by the unbeliever. Unbelievers do not understand why you are reading this book. In the vast majority of homes in America, the television is going full blast. Many of the worldly people, and some of the Christians, too, are very enamoured of those television programs, greatly thrilled by them; and they would rather be entertained by them than to read this book about the word of God.

But I have written this book, and you are reading it. You and I take time to contact the Lord. You and I have his life in us, and we see him.

That is the hidden life of the believer. The world does not understand it, but we do. It is a resurrection, a quickening, an opening, a sensitivity. And finally, it is glory; it is heaven; it is Jesus.

The King IS Coming

"When Jesus, who is our life, shall appear, then shall ye also appear with him in glory." Now this is something stated as a fact. There is no arguing this; the Bible does not discuss it or defend it. It is simply stated.

The apostle does the same sort of declaration that the first verse of the Bible does: "In the beginning God." You can search through the Bible from cover to cover to see if there is a discussion about whether God exists, but you will not find such a discussion. The Bible does not discuss this matter. It states it in Genesis 1:1 and goes on from there. The fact is, God *is*. That is not debatable.

And Paul does the same thing here about our Lord's coming: "When Christ, who is our life, shall appear." He just states it; he does not argue it, nor does he defend it. He just declares it.

This new appearance of Christ which the apostle has declared, and which we are expecting, is a new *kind* of appearance. We have not seen Christ manifested in his glory, other than in the quick scene of the transfiguration. It is said in the Scriptures that in Christ God was manifest in the flesh. That is true, but it is also true that the flesh shrouded and veiled God's glory. You will find the phrase, "The veil of his flesh" in the Scriptures. When that veil was broken—pulled apart—we saw Christ's glory and his entrance into heaven for us.

God was certainly manifested in the flesh, as the Scriptures say, but that same flesh also veiled the real glory of the Lord. Outside of the transfiguration, when that glory for a moment broke through, the real glory of Jesus, God manifest, was never seen during his earthly career.

There is a special meaning in the Greek word *parousia* which is translated "appearing." We should realize that *parousia* has never yet been fulfilled. There is to be a greater glory than we have yet perceived. There is to be a splendor, a *Shekinah*, a revelation of God in Christ that the world has never imagined. And it will happen on that glorious and final day when the Lord himself shall appear in all of the light and glory of heaven—"When Christ, who is our life, shall appear."

Now, how exactly will he appear? The Scriptures avow that he will appear personally, in resplendent glory, in iridescent, indescribable beauty, the wonder of all God's heaven. He shall surely appear gloriously.

But some people may say, "That means spiritually, not personally and actually and really. Christ will appear spiritually. Because they do not really believe in an actual physical coming of the Lord, they spiritualize, or conceptualize his appearing. But understand this: Christ is already here spiritually.

When we observe the Lord's Supper, when we keep the ordinance of baptism, when we teach and preach to the people, Jesus says, "Lo, I am with you alway, even unto the end of the world."

When we have the Lord's Supper, Jesus is with us spiritually. He is in our midst. But see what he says: "For as often as ye eat this bread, and drink this cup, ye do shew the Lord's death till he come." Thus, there must be another coming, a second coming. There is another appearing that will do away with the Lord's Supper. We simply will not need it any longer. Christ is with us *spiritually* now; he will be with us in *visible presence* in the future.

The Lord's Supper serves now to remind us of his wounds, his blood, his suffering, his scars. But obviously when the next coming is accomplished, when there is this other "appearing," we will not need to be reminded of those things. They will have been fulfilled, and the Lord will be with us in reality.

He shall appear personally. He shall appear, in his word, as a thief in the night, as if to steal away his jewels. All of us will be caught up then with the Lord into glory. Many of the parables served to explain how, like a thief in the night, the Lord will come to steal away his jewels; when both the wise and the foolish virgins are asleep; when the steward, thinking the Lord delays his coming, begins to be drunken and to beat his fellow stewards; when all cry peace and safety, then will the Lord come like a thief in the night.

Now let us understand this. He shall also come openly and publicly; just as lightning crosses the sky, so shall the Lord be seen in life and in glory coming literally with his holy angels and with his saints. And at that time also is our true appearance before the world with Christ. In both the rapture of the church, the catching up of the saints, and in the second coming when Christ returns to the earth, he will appear literally, in reality, and he will be seen. "When Christ, who is our life, shall appear, then shall ye also appear with him in glory." We will be taken away to meet the Lord in the air to begin with, and then come back with the Lord in the clouds of heaven with all of his holy angels, at the second coming.

The Blessed Hope

"Then shall ye also appear with him in glory." The manifestation of the life of Christ is the manifestation of our own lives. We are one with him. If he is glorified, we shall be glorified. If he is raised, we will be raised. If he lives, we shall live. If he comes again, we shall come with him. If he shall never die, we shall never die. If he is in heaven, we shall be in heaven. If he is honored by those of the celestial host, we shall be honored as kings and priests to God our Father forever and ever.

We will do what Christ will do. We are in him and he is in us.

We shall appear with him when he comes in glory. Each believer is like a simple little acorn. In that acorn, hidden away, are all the branches and glory of the mighty oak. All that the tree will ever be is hidden away in that acorn. All of the glory and life and immortality that is our due are hidden away in us to be manifested, to be revealed at that day, at that hour, at that time when Christ comes.

As of now we are like eagles, but trapped and chained to the earth. We are as if able to fly, were it not for that remorseless chain. We lift up our faces to heaven, looking into the sun, into the blue of God's sky, but as yet we cannot fly. How we would soar, how we would live, how

we would be with God if we but could! But we are chained
for the moment in this body of mortality and death.

But someday, some glorious and incomparable day, God
shall liberate us. He will break that earthly chain. Body
and spirit shall be made immortal and glorified like our
own living Savior, and we shall be as he is "when Christ,
who is our life, shall appear."

What a word, what a hope, what a faith, what a message,
what a promise! But the man who does not see it, and
who cannot find it because his eyes are closed to it, simply
dies. The world has seized him, Satan has blinded him,
and he turns aside from the living Lord. Thus he dies,
and he dies yet again. He dies in the flesh in this life,
and then later on he dies the second death, he dies in
his soul. He dies, shut out from God. He dies away from
Christ. He dies in the darkness of damnation, in the pit
of perdition and hell. He dies, and he dies.

Dear God, what a burden! How could a man even think
of it? How could a man dare to mention it, were it not
for the love of God that would reveal such a fate to a
soul lest he fall and perish? How could we even contemplate damnation without knowing there is a solution? How
could we think of being pure nothingness and live with
that thought if there were not another way provided by
God?

It is so plain. We each need to look to Jesus. We need
to hide our lives in the heart of Jesus until the time of
his appearing. We lose everything if we fail to do that.

We certainly need to turn aside from the call of the
world and listen to the call of Jesus. We need to make
a confession of him openly and boldly. We need to follow
him. We need to be baptized in obedience to his command
and raised in the likeness of his resurrection.

Logically and obviously all of us need to sit down and

consider our fate. Do we really believe in his future appearing? Are we really looking for him? Do we have that blessed hope in our hearts?

According to the word of God, each man's decision on this point determines his future for all eternity.

5
The King and
the Kingdom

What would it be like to see God Almighty sitting on his throne in heaven?

Has any man seen what God's own throne room looks like and how our Father in heaven appears there in glory?

Actually, if we look into the book of Revelation and the faithful reporting of the apostle John, we have pictured for us God's throne room. John, exiled to a lonely island, has seen and has preserved for us the stunning scene of Almighty God on his throne.

John writes: "And he that sat was to look upon like a jasper and a sardine stone: and there was a rainbow round about the throne, in sight like unto an emerald" (Rev. 4:3).

An exposition of this remarkable verse in all its fullness would be a weighty chapter indeed. But I wish to concentrate on one inspired symbol which John includes in his description of God's throne in heaven. John sees the throne of the Lord God Almighty, and around it he sees a full rainbow.

That rainbow represents our covenant-keeping God. The covenant promises that God has made, he certainly will faithfully perform.

The most sweeping covenant that God ever made was the one he made with Abraham, and the entire Bible following the twelfth chapter of Genesis is a working out, a fulfillment in destiny and in history, of that promise. That contract with Abraham is repeated several times in the Scriptures. The last time it is specifically given is in Genesis 22:16-18: "By myself have I sworn, saith the Lord, for because thou hast done this thing, and has not withheld thy son, thine only son: that in blessing I will bless thee, and in multiplying I will multiply thy seed as the stars of the heaven, and as the sand which is upon the sea shore; and thy seed shall possess the gate of his enemies; and in thy seed shall all the nations of the earth be blessed."

The Seed of Abraham

The expression "the seed of Abraham" refers to three separate entities. First, it obviously refers to the posterity, the descendants of Abraham. It refers to the Hebrew nation, the Israelite people. And the Lord actually swears, saying, "I will bless thee, and . . . I will multiply thy seed as the stars of the heaven, and as the sand which is upon the sea shore" (Gen. 22:17). So the seed refers first to the descendants of the patriarchs, to the Hebrew people.

The New Testament letters are addressed to the Hebrew people, as in James 1:1, "James, a servant of God and of the Lord Jesus Christ, to the twelve tribes which are scattered abroad, greeting." Again, in 1 Peter 1:1, "Peter, an apostle of Jesus Christ, to the strangers scattered throughout Pontus and Galatia, Cappadocia, Asia, and Bithynia."

In the Bible there is no such thing as ten lost tribes, we should recognize. That comes out of somebody's unscriptural imagination. In Revelation 7, we see that God will seal 12,000 from each one of the twelve tribes of Israel in coming times (vv. 4-7). Men may have lost track of ten tribes, but God has not lost them. Men are not aware of where all of the tribal Jews are located, nor which man belongs to which tribe. But God knows. And God said to Abraham, "In blessing I will bless thee, and . . . I will multiply thy seed as the stars of the heaven and as the sand which is upon the sea shore."

It goes without saying that God, Creator of all of the stars in the sky and each grain of sand on the seashore, is aware of the location of each of the twelve tribes and each of their members.

Secondly, Abraham's seed refers to his *spiritual* seed. Galatians 3 concludes, "There is neither Jew nor Greek, there is neither bond nor free, there is neither male nor female: for ye are all one in Christ Jesus. And if ye be Christ's, then are ye Abraham's seed, and heirs according to the promise" (vv. 28-29). Now certainly that does not mean there are not now any men and women. And it does not mean that there are no Jews and no Greeks anymore. In every city of the world you will meet Greeks (Gentiles), and you will likely meet Jews. But in this era in which we live, this age of grace, there is in Christ Jesus a great fellowship, his "called-out" people, his church. And that fellowship in Christ overwhelms the physical distinctions between human beings. That fellowship in Christ is Abraham's seed and the heirs according to the promise. Spiritually, even the distinction between male and female is subordinate to the distinction between the called-out people and the others.

The third meaning of Abraham's seed is simply "seed," singular. "And in thy seed shall all the nations of the earth be blessed" (Gen. 22:18). In Galatians 3:16 Paul wrote: "Now to Abraham and his seed were the promises made. He saith not, And to seeds, as of many; but as of one, And to thy seed, which is Christ." Here Abraham's seed is Christ, the messianic hope, that great Lord and coming

King.

We hark back to the beginning of the Bible, that familiar refrain that began in the Garden of Eden and reaches out to the great climactic triumph of all time and of all history. Genesis 3 refers to the seed of the woman.

Jesus and the Kingdom

In the Garden of Eden, God said to the serpent, "I will put enmity between thee and the woman, and between thy seed and her seed; it shall bruise thy head, and thou shalt bruise his heel" (Gen. 3:15). The old rabbis pored over that subtle Scripture through the millennia: the seed of the woman.

After all, a woman does not have a seed. A man has the seed. But the seed of the woman shall crush Satan's head, or so God said. Thus as this unfolding is first made, whoever he is is to be born of a woman and not of a man. This is to be remarkable "seed" indeed. He is to be delivered of a virgin.

In Genesis 12:1-3 we read that the Lord said to Abram, get out of this land to one I will show you, and I'll make of you a great nation, and in you and in your seed shall all the nations of the earth be blessed. Then the Coming One is going to be a Hebrew and not a Gentile. He will be born to a Jew.

In Genesis 21:12 we see further, "In Isaac shall thy seed be called." Abraham had intreated God on behalf of Ishmael, his firstborn, but here God makes clear that the "seed" is going to be born of Isaac and not of Ishmael.

In Genesis 28:1-4 we gather further specifics about this great covenant concerning the Messiah. "And Isaac called Jacob, and blessed him, and charged him, and said unto him . . . God Almighty bless thee, and make thee fruitful . . . and give thee the blessing of Abraham, to thee, and to thy seed with thee; that thou mayest inherit the land wherein thou art a stranger, which God gave unto Abraham." Thus the seed is going to be born of Israel, and not of Edom, the land of Esau, Jacob's brother. God continually narrows and specifies the ancestry of the seed, the Messiah.

Continuing in Genesis 49:8-10, "Judah, thou art he whom thy brethren shall praise. . . . Judah is a lion's whelp. . . . The scepter shall not depart from Judah, nor a lawgiver from between his feet, until Shiloh come; and unto him shall the gathering of the people be." This narrows the ancestry of the Messiah to the tribe of Judah and not, say, of Simeon or Levi. It might have seemed as though he would have come out of the seed of Joseph, for Joseph inherited the birthright. But the seed is to come out of Judah; and further, Judah shall be the seat of the government until Shiloh—until the messianic promise is fulfilled.

In 1 Samuel 16:1, and more clearly in Micah 5:2, we learn that he is to be born in Bethlehem; he is to born in the house of Judah, in the family of Jesse. And he is not to be of the firstborn, and not of Abinadab the second-born, and not of the third-born, but he is to be born of David. In 2 Samuel 7:12-13, 16, God said to David, "When thy days be fulfilled, and thou shalt sleep with thy fathers, I will set up thy seed after thee, which shall proceed out of thy bowels, and I will establish his kingdom. . . . I will stablish the throne of his kingdom for ever." A seed as of one, said God to David, and he shall reign forever and forever.

All through the Bible we see that "seed" promise reaffirmed and repeated. In Psalm 89:3-4: "I have made a covenant with my chosen. . . . Thy seed will I establish for ever" and continuing in verses 20,24,34, and 36. More of the same message is found in Jeremiah 23:5-6 and

34:20-23. Isaiah sings of it, too. Thus throughout does the Bible proclaim the coming of the King.

But some say that this is merely an Old Testament philosophy, a part of the old covenant. There was a king coming then, and there was a kingdom promised back then, but the New Testament changed all that. There is not to be a king and a historically manifested kingdom. The New Testament gives a different message, they say. They imply that God has changed, that he has forgotten the thing he wrote before. The New Testament gives a new philosophy, they say.

But read the word of the Lord! In Luke 1:31-33 we read almost the exact same words as we read in the Old Testament. There are a multitude of New Testament passages whereby God swears that the seed of David, the son born of a woman of the tribe of Judah, shall establish his throne forever and shall reign over God's people on the earth. God promised a kingdom, and our coming King shall establish it and reign forever and ever.

Think of the story of the mother of Zebedee's children in Matthew 20:20 and following. She wanted her sons to sit at Jesus' right hand and left hand in the kingdom to come. We can certainly understand her sentiments. In this day and age we might often hear a mother wish that one of her sons could be the Secretary of State and the other the Treasurer of the United States. We can't blame her for wanting the best for her boys. Jesus did not chide her; for a mother to be ambitious for her children is a fine thing.

But what an opportune time for Jesus to explain, "Now you do not understand. There is not going to be any manifested historical kingdom. I have changed all that." But Jesus never said anything like that. He had been preaching the kingdom. He had made it very clear that his kingdom was to come. He had his disciples pray that it might come. He said to this precious mother, "I can't give you the seat on my right hand and the seat on my left hand, but there *is* a seat on my right hand in that kingdom, and there *is* a seat on my left hand in that kingdom, and it will be given to those for whom it is prepared of my Father." Jesus left no doubt that there was indeed a kingdom to come.

Jesus said, "I was born a King." "Art thou the King of the Jews?" asked Pilate of Jesus. "Thou sayest," Jesus replied. The most definite and strongest affirmation in the Greek language is utilized by Jesus when he says, "Thou sayest." We might use the more up-to-date expression "You said it!"

Just before he died, in that awful and tragic night described in Luke 22:30, Jesus said, "I appoint unto you a kingdom, as my father has appointed unto me; that ye may eat and drink at my table in my kingdom, and sit on thrones judging the twelve tribes of Israel." Jesus had said much the same thing to his disciples in Matthew 19:28.

Our hearts go out to the thief on the cross, crucified next to Jesus, an ignorant, uncouth, rude villain, a malefactor, hated of men. But he had obviously heard the message of Jesus, and when he bowed his head to die he turned to the Lord and said, "Lord, remember me when thou comest into thy kingdom." Where did this common thief get the message about a coming kingdom that has eluded even some studied theologians of our own time? How did he come to imagine that Jesus, the man hanging on the next cross, could take him to a great kingdom to come? With his own minor acquaintance with the message and ministry of our Lord, this thief knew him as a king and counted on a coming kingdom.

Would God that we could all realize with that thief that

the promises of God never fail!

In Acts 1 Jesus is about to ascend to his father, to be received by a cloud into heaven, and his disciples questioned him quickly about the kingdom to come. Would he establish it right now, they wanted to know (Acts 1:6). Again Jesus has the opportunity to explain that there just is not going to be any kingdom. He could have said, "I have changed all those promises into spiritual promises only. God makes promises, but he doesn't keep them in the same way that he makes them. He is not able to carry through in a historical fulfillment."

But Jesus did not say that to the disciples. Why did Jesus not say that? The Lord Jesus reflects the Lord God himself. He is called the Word of God, the expression of God. And it was in the power and strength of Deity that the original covenant was made. So it will be in the power and strength of the same Lord God Almighty that that covenant is faithfully kept. Christ replied, "You are asking when the kingdom will be restored to Israel. Israel *has* a part in it, but you are not to know the time. The Father has that in his own hands. But it *is* coming."

Now it is true that we don't know just when the kingdom is coming, and we have no clue anywhere in the Word of God concerning the length of this present age of grace. But make no mistake, we do know this: the King is coming, and so is his kingdom.

Why Did He Leave Us Here?

The disciples naturally wanted the kingdom immediately. Again in Acts 1 we can sympathize with their question, "Lord, wilt thou at this time restore again the kingdom to Israel?" (v. 6). The men who are asking that question had been with Jesus since the days of John the Baptist. The qualification for an apostle was first that he be associated with Jesus from the time he was baptized by John the Baptist (Acts 1:21-22). They had traveled with Jesus from the beginning days of his public ministry. They had seen his miracles, heard his sayings, witnessed the mind of Christ in action. Finally, they had suffered through his crucifixion, and with incredulous joy celebrated his resurrection.

For forty days they had been faithfully taught the meaning of the Scriptures as Christ unfolded mysteries concerning himself out of the Pentateuch, the Psalms, and the Prophets. In all of his teaching, from his baptism to the ascension in Acts 1, there had been nothing said or done by the Lord Jesus Christ that left the slightest doubt of his return and a coming kingdom. And so the disciples were eager, and they asked him about that kingdom.

"Lord, when?" Notice that they do not ask "if," but rather, "when?"

The Lord told them, "It is not for you to know when. That belongs in God's hands. *But this is what you are to do:* You are to be witnesses unto me in Jerusalem, Judea, Samaria, and to the uttermost parts of the earth."

Jesus left us here for a purpose. We are to be proclaimers of the glorious good news of salvation. We are to do this everywhere, to the ends of the earth.

We are not, it should be understood, helping to usher in the coming kingdom. When the kingdom comes, it will come by the intervention of God in history. His own strong and mighty power will establish his righteousness in this earth. But until that time comes we are to be continuing our witness, calling men to faith in Jesus. Our good works and our faithful service do not bring in the kingdom. But our witness, our preaching to the world the unsearchable riches of the love and forgiveness of God in Christ Jesus, continually enrolls subjects for the future King.

Paul, mighty missionary that he was, had much to say about this ministry of witness. In the third chapter of Ephesians he describes a mystery that no Old Testament prophet ever saw. It was a thing hidden in the heart of God. God has a dispensation of grace and forgiveness, an entire age where sins are remembered no more. All of the believers are in one body, in the fellowship of the saints, in the circle and communion of the precious body of Jesus our Lord. This age of the grace and goodness of God was not seen by the prophets.

But the kingdom to come, where is it? Is this earth forever to go on as it is now? Will sin reign forever? Is death forever to be here with us?

Has God cast away his people? Paul exclaims in Romans 11, and he answers this absurdity, "God forbid." Then he goes on to explain, "For I also am an Israelite, of the seed of Abraham" (v. 1). And he explains about the church age, the great purpose of God toward the world outside Israel. I would not have you to be ignorant of this great purpose of God previously kept secret in his heart. There is a set time known only to God, and when that last Gentile comes down the aisle, and when that last elected soul is converted, and God checks his name in the Lamb's Book of Life; when that day comes, then shall arise that great denouement and that great consummation of all history. "And so all Israel shall be saved: as it is written, There shall come out of Sion [Zion] the Deliverer, and shall turn away ungodliness from Jacob: for this is my covenant unto them, when I shall take away their sins. As concerning the gospel, they are enemies for your sakes: but as touching the election [the sovereign purpose of God], they are beloved for the fathers' sakes. For the gifts and calling of God are without repentance" (Rom. 11:26-29).

In that great and final coming and in that future kingdom, God's elect people, Israel, shall have a place and a part. A believing nation shall be born in a day. As the Lord Christ appeared to Paul, so he shall appear to his brethren after the flesh, and they will look upon their Messiah and shall mourn because of their years of rejection and unbelief. Like the brethren of the Lord who in his lifetime refused to believe on him, they shall turn and be saved. I believe the Bible teaches that in that final kingdom, Israel shall have a part.

We go to the very end of the Bible to find the story of the consummation of the kingdom of Christ. After so much previous description, the Bible is brief and magnificently incisive about the coming of the King: "I saw heaven opened, and behold a white horse; and he that sat upon him was called Faithful and True. . . . His eyes were as a flame of fire, and on his head were many crowns. . . . And he was clothed with a vesture dipped in blood: and his name is called the Word of God" (Rev. 19:11-13).

The armies of heaven that will follow Christ at that incredible moment are God's saints, the believers, dressed in fine linen pure and white. And out of his mouth comes that word of rule and authority by which he shall judge the earth and tread the winepress of the fierceness and wrath of Almighty God.

It will be most clear to the world who it is making that stupendous entrance. "And he hath on his vesture and on his thigh a name written, KING OF KINGS, AND LORD OF LORDS" (Rev. 19:16).

The devil will at last get his due: "And I saw an angel come down from heaven, having the key of the bottomless pit and a great chain in his hand. And he laid hold on the dragon, that old serpent, which is the Devil, and Satan, and bound him a thousand years" (Rev. 20:1-2).

Thrones are then described, and on them God's sainted

people reigning with their King.

That is when God's will shall be done on earth as it is in heaven. That is when the wolf shall lie down with the lamb. That is when the lion will eat straw like an ox. That is when we will have peace on earth, goodwill toward men.

The King and the kingdom! "That's what it's all about," in today's expression. That is the Bible; that is the hope; that is the blessedness that awaits us. That is our Savior fulfilling his promises as we always knew in our hearts he would.

6
Until the Lord Come

After such good news of the King and his coming kingdom, we must now open the Bible to a place of divisiveness in the Christian church. It seemed that the believers in Corinth had been listening to a variety of preachers and had divided into groups, each following their favorite.

Some of the Corinthians had listened to Apollos preach, and some had listened to Cephas (Simon Peter), and some to Paul. Each group seemed to judge the preachers, and there was dissension in the church.

The Corinthians had managed to form cliques, and the cliques stood against each other.

Thus, Paul begins the fourth chapter of 1 Corinthians by saying, "Let a man so account of us, as ministers of Christ, and stewards of the mysteries of God. Moreover it is required in stewards, that a man be found faithful. But with me it is a very small thing that I should be judged by you or by any man's judgment" (vv. 1-3).

There is an interesting Greek phrase in that verse: *anthrōpinēs hēmeras*. The word for "man" in Greek is *anthropos*, and *anthrōpinēs* means "human." Now the Greek word for "day" is *hēmera*. So to translate the Greek there more literally: "that I should be judged of you or of man's days *(anthrōpinēs hēmeras)*." The context leads me to believe that he evidently has in mind the same idea

he expressed in Romans 3:13—"Every man's work shall
be made manifest: for the day shall declare it." That day
is the day of the Lord. Paul says man's day and man's
judgment is comparatively meaningless. What a man thinks
about me, Paul says, means nothing to me. What men's
courts might judge concerning me is irrelevant. "Yea, I
judge not mine own self. For I know nothing by myself;
yet am I not hereby justified: but he that judgeth me is
the Lord" (Rom. 4:3-4). What men think is as changeable
as the weather. One day up, one day down, one time this,
one time that. One day the mob shouts "Hosannah!" to
the Son of David, and the next day they say, "Crucify
him, crucify him!"

That is a sad but typical example of men's judgment.

Paul says plainly that men's opinions and judgments
amount to nothing. He says: yea. even my own judgment
concerning myself is nothing, for even though I may not
know anything against myself, yet I am not thereby justified. But there is one that judges me, the Lord! "Therefore, judge nothing before the time, until the Lord come,
who both will bring to light the hidden things of darkness,
and will make manifest the counsels of the hearts: and
then shall every man have praise of God" (Rom. 4:5).

Clearly we understand that we are to judge nothing
before the Lord comes. Obviously the judgment of the
Lord is what counts and what will be accurate, and the
matter of judgment of other men, and even of ourselves,
is simply not up to us.

It is clear that Paul is not teaching here about the return
of the Lord. In point of fact, the glory of our Lord's return
comes in only incidentally. As the chapter goes on, Paul
changes subjects and talks about something else. And that
is the beauty of this particular lesson by Paul—that the
Lord's coming is only incidentally mentioned; that he

assumes it to be *fact*, and that he knows his readers assume it to be fact.

My thesis is this: that the background against which all of these writings in the Bible have been drawn—the background against which all of the revelations of God are made—is that Christ is coming again.

An example of that great background of Scripture is in our ordinance of the Lord's Supper. In 1 Corinthians 11:26, Paul quotes the Lord as saying, "For as often as ye eat this bread, and drink this cup, ye do shew the Lord's death till he come." We break bread and share the cup against the *background* of the great coming of our glorious God and Savior, our Lord Jesus Christ. If in the Bible Paul makes an appeal that you be a follower of him even as he is a follower of Christ, he will make it as he does in Philippians 3:17,20: "Be followers together of me. . . . For our conversation is in heaven; from whence also we look for the Saviour, the Lord Jesus Christ."

Inevitably, our doctrine, our beliefs, our way of walking in the Lord is laid in bold relief against the future return of the Lord.

If the Bible lays before your heart the persuasion that you ought to live godly and walk circumspectly in this world, it will be against that same backdrop. For example in Titus 2:13, "Looking for that blessed hope, and the glorious appearing of the great God and our Saviour Jesus Christ." If there is comfort at the side of the grave of your loved one, it will be made against that same great background.

"But I would not have you to be ignorant, brethren, concerning them which are asleep, that ye sorrow not, even as others which have no hope. For if we believe that Jesus died and rose again, even so them also which sleep in

Jesus will God bring with him. For this we say unto you by the word of the Lord, that we which are alive and remain unto the coming of the Lord shall not prevent them which are asleep. For the Lord himself shall descend from heaven with a shout, with the voice of the archangel, and with the trump of God: and the dead in Christ shall rise first: Then we which are alive and remain shall be caught up together with them in the clouds, to meet the Lord in the air: and so shall we ever be with the Lord. Wherefore comfort one another with these words" (1 Thess. 4:13-18).

That is true comfort, even at the side of the grave of a loved one, and again the comfort is in the coming of the King. (We have submitted these verses previously in another context, and will again before this book is done. But no one has ever seen the Scripture that can be read too often.)

Even if there is an appeal in the Bible to people who are troubled, it will be made in the light of the return of the Lord Jesus. In 2 Thessalonians 1:7-8: "You who are troubled rest with us, when the Lord Jesus shall be revealed from heaven with his mighty angels, in flaming fire taking vengeance on them that know not God, and that obey not the gospel of our Lord Jesus Christ." If there is the admonition on the part of the apostle that we preach the word, that we be true to the Book, he will make it on the basis of the return of the Lord.

Second Timothy 4:1-2 puts it, "I charge thee therefore before God, and the Lord Jesus Christ, who shall judge the quick and the dead at his appearing and his kingdom; preach the word." It is invariably against the background of that great and final and consummating event, of the return of the Lord, that all of these appeals are made in the Word of God.

All of the prophets (as well as the Lord Jesus himself),

and all of the apostles lift their voices with unanimity of heart and testimony to that glorious and final time. First, consider the witness of the Lord Jesus himself speaking in John 14:1-3: "Let not your heart be troubled: ye believe in God, believe also in me. In my Father's house are many mansions: if it were not so, I would have told you. I go to prepare a place for you. And if I go and prepare a place for you, I will come again, and receive you unto myself; that where I am, there ye may be also."

Consider the witness of the angels from heaven. In Acts 1:11, the angel said to the disciples, "Ye men of Galilee, why stand ye gazing up into heaven? this same Jesus, which is taken up from you into heaven, shall so come in like manner as ye have seen him go into heaven." It is the testimony of the preaching of Simon Peter in Acts 3:19-21. In his sermon the apostle says, "Repent ye therefore, and be converted, that your sins may be blotted out, when the times of refreshing shall come from the presence of the Lord; and he shall send Jesus Christ, which before was preached unto you: whom the heaven must receive until the times of restitution of all things, which God hath spoken by the mouth of all his holy prophets since the world began."

Paul's first letter to the Corinthians is replete with such examples: "Even as the testimony of Christ was confirmed in you: so that ye come behind in no gift; waiting for the coming of our Lord Jesus Christ" (1:6). And this letter to that divisive church ends with a stunning phrase: "If any man love not the Lord Jesus Christ, let him be Ana-thema Maranatha. The grace of our Lord Jesus be with you. . . . Amen" (16:22-24). *Maranatha* is an Aramaic word meaning "the Lord comes." Paul's conclusion in his letter to the Corinthians was again a reference to the con-summation of all history, the coming of the Lord.

Examples continue throughout the writing of all of the

witnesses of the Bible. In Hebrews: "And as it is appointed
unto men once to die, but after this the judgment: So Christ
was once offered to bear the sins of many; and unto them
that look for him shall he appear the second time without
sin unto salvation" (9:27-28). James, the pastor of the first
church at Jerusalem and half-brother of our Lord, says,
"Be ye also patient; stablish your hearts: for the coming
of the Lord draweth nigh" (Jas. 5:8). James' own brother
(also a half-brother of the Lord Jesus) Jude, in the fourteenth verse of his little epistle, says, "Behold, the Lord
cometh with ten thousands of his saints." And what could
I say of the book of the Revelation, whose great theme
is manifested in Revelation 1:5-7? "Unto him that loved
us, and washed us from our sins in his own blood, and
hath made us kings and priests unto God and his Father;
to him be glory and dominion for ever and ever. Amen.
Behold, he cometh with clouds; and every eye shall see
him, and they also which pierced him: and all kindreds
of the earth shall wail because of him."

The great theme of the whole Bible is this: In the Old
Testament: Somebody is coming. In the Gospels: Somebody has come. In the Epistles and the Revelation: Somebody is coming again. He who was to come, he who has
come, and he who is returning once again! And that is
all there is to that.

And the Bible itself concludes on the last page with
the revealed Lord Jesus promising, "Surely I come
quickly," and the answer of John the apostle and of all
of the people of God of the ages is, "Even so come, Lord
Jesus" (Rev. 22:20).

The Return of the Lord

There are three elements concerning the return of the
Lord which we should keep in mind. First, he is coming

actually, literally, visibly, openly, bodily, physically. Second, he shall reign over an actual, visible, literal kingdom. Third, we shall be citizens of that kingdom as actual, physical, resurrected, immortalized, glorified people.

We have previously discussed the Greek word that is used in the New Testament for the return of the Lord, that word, *parousia*. And we have stressed that this very common word has one meaning, and one meaning only. It denotes a physical, bodily presence. In no place, in no passage, in no example is it, nor can it ever be, used figuratively or spiritually. The word *parousia* refers to a physical, bodily presence.

It is not just in connection with Christ that *parousia* refers to a bodily presence. True enough, the disciples asked him, "What shall be the sign of thy coming [*parousia*]"; and the Lord told them, "For as the lightning cometh out of the east, and shineth even unto the west; so shall also the [*parousia*] of the Son of man be" (Matt. 24:3,27). And the Lord went on to refer to the days of Noah, and "So shall also the [*parousia*] of the Son of man be" (v. 37). So, *parousia* refers to a physical, bodily presence in connection with *anybody*, not just the Son of God.

We should realize that we do not arrive at this doctrine about a physical and real coming simply because we are dealing with Christ. We should realize that the apostle Paul utilizes the same term, *parousia*, in connection with ordinary, earthly events.

In 2 Corinthians 10:10, Paul quotes his enemies; he is discussing what his enemies say about him and he writes, "For his [Paul's] letters are weighty and powerful; but his bodily presence [*parousia*] is weak, and his speech contemptible." That is what Paul's enemies said about him, and we can certainly gather that they did not appreciate the man for what he was. But our point here is that the word *parousia* is no magic word. In this particular connection it simply means that Paul did not make a very powerful appearance. He looked like nothing very impressive.

In Philippians 2:12 we have another example: "Wherefore, my beloved, as ye have always obeyed, not as in my presence [*parousia*] only, but now much more in my absence, work out your own salvation with fear and trembling." *Parousia*, we might say, is no respecter of persons; it is simply applied to *anyone's* actual, physical presence.

Now it should be understood that the Bible is not written in some special kind of language all of its own. As a matter of fact, it is in the *Koine* Greek, as we have seen. There was a time a few generations ago when people thought, and scholars said, that the Bible was written more or less in its own language. But in the last several years, archaeologists digging in the hermetically sealed ash-heaps and dump-heaps that surrounded the great cities of Egypt have found some interesting evidence along these lines. The scientists have found papyri by the thousands and thousands, protected from the inclement Mediterranean weather by being sealed under sand or under stone. We have now been able to compare Bible manuscripts, written in what is called the *hagio-koine-dialectus*, the common vernacular of the early Christian people. And the startling thing is that the common, everyday Greek of those papyri is the same as the Greek of the New Testament. Love letters have been found, legal proceedings, documents of all sorts; and all of that and more was written on papyri *in the language of the New Testament*. The New Testament clearly was written in a vernacular language, a language that all of the people understood and used daily. The meanings of its words were quite clear, and normally quite simple.

We are interested in the use of the word, *parousia*,

obviously, to see if it might apply in everyday cases. Does it always mean the physical presence of the individual? We saw that *parousia* is used in connection with the Lord, indicating his physical presence. But then he is the Son of God, after all. We further saw that this was used of Paul by his detractors, but then Paul was an apostle. Perhaps he, too, was a special case. But in the papyri, the common papers, letters, and documents of a vast civilization of Greek-speaking people, we would expect to find no special biases. And the word *parousia* appears again and again.

There are three instances out of a thousand that we might look at to show the common meaning of the term *parousia.* There was a certain woman named Dionysia, who was fighting a lawsuit before the prefect of the district in which she made her home. As the trial dragged on, she petitioned the court for permission to return home on the grounds that the care of her property demanded her *parousia,* and she could not administer her estate while absent.

A second instance gives the account of a royal visit by Ptolemy to a certain district which had been taxed outrageously to raise funds to pay for his entertainment during his *parousia* in the region (during his personal visit, his bodily presence in the region). Another one of those papyri describes the preparation for a festival in behalf of the governor upon his *parousia.*

The point is clear. *Parousia* meant simply, to anyone who read it, the physical, actual presence of the individual concerned. As surely as the embattled landlady and the high-living politicians were referred to as real people with real presences, the Lord shall come in reality.

Jesus was not a spirit. He lived in a body. He had bones, he had flesh, he grew tired and hungry, and he wept. He was somebody, just like you and I are somebody.

Everybody has to have a place to be, and Jesus presently lives in a *topos*. That is the Greek term in the fourteenth chapter of John: "I go to prepare a place [*topos*] for you" (v. 2). A body has to have a place, and heaven is a place for people, and the Lord Jesus is a person. He is somebody, and he is coming again, visibly, literally, actually, physically.

His *parousia* is expected in the normal, everyday sense of the term *parousia*. The Lord Jesus shall appear someday.

The Reign of the King

Many people fail to picture that Jesus will reign over an actual kingdom. He will run an actual government. He will be the head of a great world theocracy. And his administration will be the fulfillment of man's dream of a utopia.

Man has always dreamed of a utopia. Ever since the days of the ancients, there has been a heartfelt desire for a perfect society. Plato's *Republic* is nothing but the philosophical description of what he considered an ideal government. Sir Thomas Moore's *Utopia* is another metaphysical approach to the longing in the hearts of men for justice and liberty. Communism has a great appeal to intellectuals who dream of a perfect government in this earth. Its promises of fair sharing among all of the society have great appeal.

But there is always a catch. All tries for a utopia have failed. We can see today the Communist's ideal and how it really works. The socialistic state that is supposed to dissolve all classes somehow comes to nothing, and worse than nothing.

The perfect government never comes to pass by men's efforts. It never will. It simply cannot. There is a wonderful story about a Communist agitator speaking to a crowd on the street. In his enthusiasm for a socialistic doctrine he spoke eloquently, and he promised, "Comrades, come the revolution and we will all eat strawberries and cream three times every day." Well, it seems one fellow in the crowd was not impressed. He spoke up and said, "But I don't like strawberries!" The speaker got red in the face, and he shook his fist in the face of the critic and said, "Come the revolution and we'll eat strawberries three times a day and *like* it!"

It is not the strawberries that frighten us so much, to be sure; it is that fist in our faces. That great socialistic utopia sometimes comes accompanied by clenched fists and secret police. We not only have to like strawberries; we also have to like everything that the central planners like.

And we certainly make mistakes, too, in capitalistic enterprises. There is something wrong with every system of government made by men. It is easy to see that there is no perfect nation, and there never has been. There simply are no perfect men. But there is coming a time, a glorious time—there is coming a day when there shall be in this earth the fulfillment of man's utopian dreams. When the King comes we shall achieve a true utopia!

In Daniel 2 we have a rather frightening image that Daniel interprets for us. There is a head of gold representing Babylon, and a breast of silver representing the Medo-Persian empire. Thighs of brass represent the Greco-Alexandrian empire. Two iron legs symbolically picture the eastern and the western Roman Empire. The toes of the image are part of iron and part of clay. What we have there is a picture of some weak nations and some strong nations, the toes, beneath the mighty empires above.

Then there comes a great rock, cut without hands, and it smites the image on those toes. And the rock grows to be a great, great kingdom that fills the whole earth. The image shows that human governments are divided. The world will never be under one human government. But the kingdom of the smiting rock, the kingdom of God which will stand forever, prevails.

That kingdom over which the Lord will actually reign is a government. "Unto us a child is born" (Isa. 9). That foretells the story of Luke. "And a son is given." That is fulfilled in John 3:16. Whoever trusts in the Son will be saved. "And the government shall be upon his shoulder." Upon the throne of David and upon his kingdom shall he establish it. He is going to be a king, a governor, a ruler. He has the names of deity. "His name shall be called Wonderful, Counsellor, the mighty God, the everlasting Father, the Prince of Peace."

And how shall this come to pass? How shall this Prince of Peace come to power? Will it be by social legislation, by economic amelioration? Perhaps by detente? Not at all. It shall come to pass by the power of God himself. "The zeal of the Lord of Hosts will perform this," the Scripture tells us. God shall do it.

Clearly, if it depended upon man to accomplish this, it would never be accomplished. It would simply never come to pass. Fortunately, "The zeal of the Lord of Hosts will perform this."

On Earth As It Is in Heaven

What a life in the kingdom to come!

God's own description is inspiring: "The wolf also shall dwell with the lamb, and the leopard shall lie down with the kid. . . . And the cow and the bear shall feed; their young ones shall lie down together: and the lion shall eat straw like the ox."

Even if man could achieve his utopia, the world will

still be filled with shed blood. The lion would still destroy his prey, and the wolf would still slay the flock. Right now if the wolf and the lamb lie down together, the lamb ends up on the inside of the wolf, and *we* cannot change that.

But in the great millennial kingdom of the Lord, there is going to be a reversal of these tragic facts of nature. God did not originally make it that way. It is not God's will for nature to be that way. In Genesis 1:29-30, "And God said, Behold, I have given you every herb bearing seed, which is upon the face of all the earth, and every tree, in the which is the fruit of a tree yielding seed; to you it shall be for meat. And to every beast of the earth, and to every fowl of the air, and to every thing that creepeth upon the earth, wherein there is life, I have given every green herb for meat: and it was so." In the days of the edenic paradise, no creature slew another creature. No animal took the life of another animal. No violence and bloodshed were in the paradise of God. It was only after sin came that the animals began to slay and to shed blood. But in this kingdom that is coming, the lion shall eat straw like the ox. The wolf and the lamb shall lie down together. In this same passage, the little babies shall play on the hole of the asp, "and the weaned child shall put his hand on the cockatrice's den. They shall not hurt nor destroy in all my holy mountain: for the earth shall be full of the knowledge of the Lord, as the waters cover the sea" (Isa. 11:8-9).

Now that is Old Testament Scripture, some say. Yes, it is. But the Old Testament is the foundation of even more glorious revelations in the New Testament. Consider Paul, saying this same thing in Romans 8:19-23. To paraphrase Paul, the earnest longing of the creation waits for the *apocalypse*, the unveiling, the revealing of the Son of

God. For the creation was made subject to violence and
to blood and to animals eating one another. The creation
was made subject to that not willingly, but by reason of
him who subjected the creation to that because of sin,
but also in hope. The hope is that the creation itself will
be "delivered from the bondage of corruption into the
glorious liberty of the children of God. For we know that
the whole creation groaneth and travaileth in pain together
until now. And not only they, but ourselves also, which
have the firstfruits of the Spirit, even we ourselves groan
within ourselves, waiting for the adoption, to wit, the redemption of our body."

We know what it is to groan under the burden of this
terrible universe in which we live. Disease and age is
pressing down upon all of us, and finally death and decay.
And what we see in ourselves we see in the whole animal
kingdom. Bloodshed and slaughter, lying in wait and in
prey! It is a world of blood and of death. But in the new
kingdom, the millennial kingdom, the glorious kingdom
over which Jesus Christ shall reign, we shall again have
back those beautiful, glorious, edenic days where the leopard and the kid lie down together, where the wolf and
the lamb are friends and neighbors, and where the lion
eats straw like an ox. All of the viciousness and hatred
and malice and blood and murder—all of it gone. Nothing
will be left except peace and righteousness, and the glory
of God in the face of Jesus Christ.

I could go on and on about our King and his coming
kingdom. The message is so clear and so gracious and
so joyous. Remember it well. He is an actual King who
is coming. And we will see him and he will reign over
an actual kingdom. And we will actually be there.

The kingdom will include actual people. You and me.
That is the greatest news of all.

7
The Day of the Lord

Judgment day!

Very few people around the world today, believing and otherwise, would fail to apprehend the general meaning of that term. Judgment day is when God will judge the world. There will come a day when men will have to own up for what they have done.

People unfamiliar with the Scriptures fail to appreciate that the idea of a judgment day is thoroughly biblical. They regard it instead as a kind of fable, a doomsday philosophy. But Paul wrote clearly to the Christians at Thessalonica about that "day of the Lord" (1 Thess. 5:1-11). He wrote many words to the wise about this culminating event in God's plan for men.

To study the background of the biblical idea of the day of the Lord involves a biblical survey from beginning to end. The Old Testament is filled with it. The prophets revealed great epochs in the destiny of mankind; and they had a phrase by which they referred to the day of judgment, the day of the wrath of God, the day of visitation from heaven, the perdition and damnation of an ungodly earth. They called it "the day of the Lord."

There is no place in the Old Testament, nor in the New Testament, where that phrase refers to any other thing but the day of tribulation, the day of wrath, the day of visitation, the day of judgment of Almighty God. The beginning of that final and terrible day of the Lord is portrayed in the sixth chapter of Revelation. The great men of the earth and the bondmen, from the slaves to the king, cry for the rocks and the mountains to hide them from the wrath of the Lamb. "For the great day of his wrath is come; and who shall be able to stand?" (Rev. 6:17).

Paul drew a distinction in 1 Thessalonians between the "day of Christ" which he covered in 1 Thessalonians 4, and the terrible "day of the Lord." The "day of Christ," literally the day of the Anointed One or Messiah, means the day of the gathering of God's children home to heaven—the day of the resurrection of the Lord's people. Having described this remarkable translation of the saints who abide and remain unto the coming of the Lord, he goes on in the fifth chapter to speak of the "day of the Lord."

Paul writes, "But of the times and the seasons, brethren, ye have no need that I write unto you" (1 Thess. 5:1). He had already told them about it.

"For yourselves know perfectly that the day of the Lord so cometh as a thief in the night. For when they shall say, Peace and safety; then sudden destruction cometh upon them, as travail upon a woman with child; and they shall not escape. But ye, brethren, are not in darkness, that that day should overtake you as a thief. Ye are all the children of light, and the children of the day: we are not of the night, nor of darkness. Therefore let us not sleep, as do others; but let us watch and be sober. For they that sleep sleep in the night; and they that be drunken are drunken in the night. But let us, who are of the day, be sober, putting on the breastplate of faith and love; and for an helmet the hope of salvation. For God hath not appointed us to wrath, but to obtain salvation by our Lord Jesus Christ, who died for us, that whether we wake or sleep, we should live together with him. Wherefore comfort yourselves together, and edify one another, even as also ye do" (vv. 2-11).

Deliverance and Vengeance

We gain a fascinating insight about the "day of the Lord" by looking into the very beginning of the public ministry of Jesus. In Luke 4 we see Jesus in Nazareth where he grew up reading the scroll of the prophet Isaiah in the synagogue. The Lord selected a hopeful passage: "The Spirit of the Lord God is upon me; because the Lord hath anointed me to preach good tidings unto the meek; he hath sent me to bind up the brokenhearted, to proclaim liberty to the captives, and the opening of the prison to them that are bound; to proclaim the acceptable year of the Lord" (Isa. 61:1-2).

Then Jesus closed the book. The Scriptures specify that he closed the book after the words "to proclaim the acceptable year of the Lord." But if we now open the book to the same passage and read over the prophecy of Isaiah, we find interestingly that the Lord chose to close the Bible in the middle of a sentence. Isaiah's passage actually concludes, "To proclaim the acceptable year of the Lord, and the day of vengeance of our God." Jesus chose not to finish with the phrase "the day of vengeance of our God." He did not read that.

We can now see why. To proclaim the acceptable year of the Lord was his first ministry. That characterized Jesus in the days of his flesh. The Lord anointed him to preach good tidings, to bind up the brokenhearted, to proclaim liberty to the captives, to proclaim the acceptable year of

the Lord. This is the day of grace. This is the day of
opportunity.

Why did Jesus not read, "and the day of vengeance
of our God"? The Lord did not read the whole sentence
because the other half of that sentence is yet to be fulfilled
in the providence and in the councils of God. First things
first; the Lord came to proclaim the kingdom of heaven
for all who would believe. There is yet coming a day of
visitation and judgment, the "day of the Lord," the "day
of the vengeance of our God."

As you read the Scriptures, you will find all through
them those two looks—a backward one and a forward one.
At the Lord's table we are eating and drinking, looking
back to the day of the Lord's goodness and kindness and
mercy in dying for our sins according to the Scriptures;
then, at the same time, we are looking forward to that
day when he comes again. And at Easter we look back
to his resurrection and forward to our own.

How wonderful it is that we have true prophecy. There
is no other religion that contains true prophecy but the
Judeo-Christian revelation. I think that is an obvious thing.
How could a Buddhist truly prophesy when the Spirit of
the Lord or the Spirit of prophecy is not upon him? How
could a Muslim, how could a Zoroastrian? But the faith
of the Lord God is the faith of the great Jehovah who
sees the end from the beginning. And things that happen
today were prophesied thousands of years ago. The denouement of all time is ever before the Lord, and he sees
it syllable by syllable, phrase and letter by phrase and
letter.

When I pick up this Holy Book, I read through the
thousands of years of the great prophecies of God fulfilled
in their time. The first coming of our Lord is spoken of
in Genesis that he should be born of a woman, a virgin-

born seed of the woman. He was to be of the seed of
Abraham, born to Judah, the fourth child of Jacob. In
the book of Samuel we read that he should be of the lineage
and of the house of David. Zechariah says that he would
present himself as the King of Israel, lowly and riding
on the foal of an ass. In the twenty-second Psalm, that
he should die on the cross, forsaken, "My God, My God."
In the sixteenth Psalm, that he should be raised from the
dead: "Thou wilt not suffer thy holy one to see corruption."
In Psalm 110, that he should be our great high priest after
the order of Melchizedek, interceding in heaven. Even the
place where he was born was prophesied 750 years before
his day. In Isaiah 6 through 9 it is prophesied that he
should be Deity himself, and his name should be called
everlasting Father, the mighty God. All of those things,
and these I have mentioned are just a few, but were fulfilled to the jot, to the tittle, to the letter, according to
the word of the prophets of God.

We should always appreciate that these great prophets,
speaking by the Spirit of God, pointed through hundreds
and thousands of years, in some instances, to such mighty
events as the first appearance of our Lord and even the
final culmination of God's plan for men. We should appreciate their accuracy, and we should take comfort that we
are not among those left "asleep." We should realize that
if the prophets accurately predicted the first appearance
of our Lord, then we can rest assured in the prophecies
concerning the second appearance of our Lord. The
prophecy of God shall never fall nor falter nor fail.

Consider for a moment the prophetic words about coming times. In Daniel 7: "I saw in the night visions, and,
behold, one like the Son of man came with the clouds
of heaven, and came to the Ancient of Days, and they
brought him near before him. And there was given him

dominion, and glory, and a kingdom, that all people, nations, and languages, should serve him: his dominion is an everlasting dominion, which shall not pass away, and his kingdom that which shall not be destroyed" (vv. 13-14). We have every cause and reason to look forward to the glorious fulfilling of the Word of the Lord.

Then again in the prophet Zechariah, the same one who prophesied of his coming, lowly, riding upon the foal of an ass, we find the prediction that "in that day . . . I will pour upon the house of David, and upon the inhabitants of Jerusalem the spirit of grace and of supplications" (12:9-10). Evidently, the house of David is going to be there in Jerusalem.

I meet many professors of theology of various stripes; and I can remember an interview with one who failed entirely to appreciate prophecy. "Does it mean nothing to you that the Amalekites and Jebusites and the Edomites and the Moabites and the Hittites and the Canaanites, and all the other ites are gone from the earth, and we have lost all trace of them? But the Israelite is still here, according to the saying of the prophet of God. Does that mean nothing to you?" "Nothing at all," he said.

"Does it mean anything to you that the prophets say, and they say and they repeat, that Israel will go back to Palestine, some of them before they are converted, and someday after they are converted all Israel will be in Palestine? Does that mean anything to you?" I asked.

"Nothing at all, nothing at all," he said.

I then asked, "Does it mean anything to you that for nearly 1,900 years there were almost no Jews in Palestine? It was a wasted and forsaken land. But according to the saying of God in the prophets who spoke of it, they are going back to their land. Is it nothing to you that today you can see Israel turning their faces toward the Holy

Land? Is that nothing to you?"

"Nothing at all," he said, "absolutely meaningless."

I thought, *Well, I'm looking at a prophecy of God itself.*
Second Peter 3 says: "There shall come in the last times
scoffers . . . saying, Where is the promise of his coming?
for since the fathers fell asleep, all things continue as they
were" (v. 3). And that professor told me, "I don't see any
sign." He doesn't know it, but he is a sign himself.

"I will pour upon the house of David, and upon the
inhabitants of Jerusalem, the spirit of grace and of supplications: and they shall look upon me whom they have
pierced, and they shall mourn for him, as one mourneth
for his only son, and shall be in bitterness for him, as
one that is in bitterness for his firstborn. In that day shall
there be a great mourning in Jerusalem. [There shall be
a mourning in every family everywhere!] In that day there
shall be a fountain opened to the house of David and
to the inhabitants of Jerusalem for sin and for uncleanness"
(Zech. 12:10;13:1). That is certainly very clear prophecy
to me. That refers to Israel, and it gives us places and
times. We can see that that is a future prophecy, and we
can see plainly what it says.

What is being said here, obviously, is that in that great
and final denouement the Lord Jesus will appear to his
people like he appeared to James, his brother, and like
he appeared to the apostle Paul, who was then Saul of
Tarsus. When Jesus appeared to Saul he was converted,
and Paul referred to himself as being "one born out of
due time" (1 Cor. 15:8), that is, before the normal time
of birth. The prophesied time for Christ's appearance to
Israel had not yet come, of course, but the Lord appeared
to him as one born "before the time."

There certainly shall be an appearing of the Lord to
his people, the Israelites, and they shall look upon him

whom they have pierced, and they shall mourn for him as one that mourns for his only son. And they shall say to him according to that same prophecy, "What are these wounds in thine hands? Then he shall answer, Those with which I was wounded in the house of my friends" (Zech. 13:6). "And his feet shall stand in that day upon the mount of Olives, which is before Jerusalem on the east, and the mount of Olives shall cleave, . . . and there shall be a very great valley" (14:4). And the prophet continues: "It shall come to pass in that day, that the light shall not be clear, nor dark. . . . At evening time it shall be light. . . . And it shall be in that day, that living waters shall go out from Jerusalem; half of them toward the former sea, and half of them toward the hinder sea. . . . And the Lord shall be king over all the earth: in that day shall there be one Lord, and his name one" (vv. 6-9). "And there shall be no more utter destruction; but Jerusalem shall be safely inhabited" (v. 11).

Now, how could we not believe in this prophecy when the very same prophet, Zechariah, along with the other prophets spoke of the first coming of our Lord in all of its humble characteristics? He did come as a Lamb of God, as a Sheep brought to the slaughter, pouring out his life for the cleansing of those who trust in him. Now, why not believe when that same prophet lifts up his voice again and proclaims these great prophecies of the denouement of the age regarding our Lord, the King of all the earth?

We have reviewed previously some of the relevant New Testament prophecies. "Ye men of Galilee, why stand ye gazing up into heaven? This same Jesus, which is taken up from you into heaven, shall so come in like manner as ye have seen him go" (Acts 1:11). And one out of a multitude of others; "Behold, he cometh with clouds; and every eye shall see him, and they also which pierced him:

and all kindreds of the earth shall wail because of him" (Rev. 1:7). This describes the beginning of the great day of the Lord when his own people who had slain him (John 1:11) will see him.

"Lord, When?"

Back to the fifth chapter of 1 Thessalonians. Paul is speaking of the time when all these prophecies will come to pass. You just cannot read these prophecies and not ask the question, "When?" When are these things to come to pass? When the disciples heard Jesus speak of these eschatological things, and when he was with them on the Mount of Olives, they asked him, saying, "Lord, when? When?" You cannot escape it, not if you are normal, and not if you are an interested Christian. So Paul attempts to answer that question—"But of the times and the seasons, brethren," you yourselves know.

Do we really know?

Paul discusses two possibilities. First, for the unconverted, the unsaved, the lost—they simply do *not* know. It is hidden from them. They are the children of darkness and they belong to the children of the night. "But of the times and the seasons, *brethren*," you do not need to have me repeat what I have already told you. "For yourselves know perfectly that the day of the Lord so cometh as a thief in the night. For when they shall say, Peace and safety; then sudden destruction cometh upon them, as travail upon a woman with child; and they shall not escape." Of that day and of that hour the lost world does not know. It is darkness to them and it is hidden away from them.

Paul gives several characteristics of the "day of the Lord" here. First, it shall come upon them without premonition, without preliminary, without sign, without program. This

great, final day of the Lord shall come suddenly and
immediately and catastrophically and finally and terribly.
Many things are said about that. We remember the parable
of the five virgins who were foolish. The five who were
wise entered into the kingdom of God, but the five who
were foolish were left outside. The Bridegroom came suddenly, and the door was shut. Just like that! They are
unprepared; they are not ready.

We remember the parable of the wicked steward. The
master of the house delayed his coming, and the steward
began to be wanton and to beat his fellow servants. In
how many instances does the Lord illustrate that? To the
unsaved it comes as a thief in the night. The image there
is of the dawn overtaking. There are thieves in the night,
and the dawn suddenly comes and overtakes them. The
world is unprepared.

Second, this great and final "day of the Lord" is going
to come at a time when the nations say we have our
protocols, we have our instruments of peace, we have the
signatures on these documents. Here is a nonagression pact.
Here is a treaty of friendship. Here is a reciprocal trade
agreement. Peace and safety!

We are today observing a tremendous paradox. The more
"united nations" we have and the more treaties we have,
the more we strive and prepare for that final and greatest
holocaust. Isn't that a strange thing? "For when they shall
say, Peace and safety" is when sudden destruction comes.
Look at this world organization. Look at this great community of nations. Look at this great stockpile of defense.
Look at all of this. Peace and safety! That identical thing
can be illustrated by the *Titanic*. The people were riding
on the bosom of the deep from Liverpool to New York
in the unsinkable *Titanic*. One moment it was unsinkable,
and the next moment it was floudering and diving and

sinking to the bottom of the North Atlantic Ocean. That is the way the biblical illustration is. The last time shall be as it was in the days of Noah. People were laughing and drinking and carrying on in a happy way in peace and safety, and then the flood came. And it shall be, the Lord says, as it was in the days of Lot. People were marrying, giving in marriage, carrying on in a great hilarious time until the fire and the brimstone fell from heaven. So it will be, he says, in this great "day of the Lord." When they shall say peace and safety, then that awful travail will come as upon a woman with birth pains, and they shall not escape.

Revelation 6 gives the same picture of suddenness. First we see the white horse, the great representative and champion of the people. Peace and safety! But then immediately thereafter, the red horse of war, the black horse of famine, and the pale horse of death. The "day of the Lord," unmistakably. It is truly sudden death.

I was in California one beautiful morning when I heard a long, mournful wail begin at exactly 11:00. It lasted for a full fifteen minutes. My curiosity got the best of me, and I asked, "What in the world is that wailing sound?" Well, it was explained to me that once a month they blow the air raid siren. The purpose is simply to acquaint the people with it. Well, I was struck by the peace and the beauty of that California morning. There was a perfectly blue sky and a lovely breeze. But then suddenly there came the alarm. I think this illustrates the point about judgment day.

Our Revelation verse gives the Greek word, *aiphnidios*, which means sudden. The word is very emphatic, and it appears first in the sentence: "Suddenly!"

The people of California hear the air raid siren, but they are not really watching for any airplanes raining death from the skies. They have become used to the siren. It is part of the life out there. But I am afraid it serves to illustrate how surprised so many people will be on that great "day of the Lord."

The Children of Light

For the lost world, for the unconverted, the "day of the Lord" certainly comes suddenly, unexpectedly, without warning. But in the next verse, the fourth verse of 1 Thessalonians 5: "But ye," you who are saved, "are not in darkness, that that day should overtake you as a thief. Ye are all the children of light, and the children of the day: we are not of the night, nor of darkness." That is, that day when it comes will not surprise *us. We* are not going to be taken aback. *We* are not going to be lost. *We* are not going to be left in the world that runs rivers of blood. Not *we.* "For God has not appointed us to wrath" (v. 9). We are not of that day of darkness that it should overtake us. We are not of that age, not of that dispensation. We are not of that judgment, of that time, of that hour. We are of the light; we are of the day. We are looking with our faces raised upward to where our Lord is in heaven. And we are not of that awful hour of darkness and damnation that it should overtake us as a thief in the night.

I cannot help but remember at this point the great national and international preachers I heard in the days of my youth, especially in New York City. Those were glamorous days of great sermons about the glories of the immediate future. Everything was just working out according to the fine genius of man, of science, of government. And everything was rosy and the millennium was right there if we were not already in it. Most of the preachers were preaching that. Then in the midst of their preaching, there came upon this world the awful blood bath of a world war. Out of the sky there rained bombs and fury. Hitler's hordes were to the east, and the conflict whirled around to the west, and we suddenly found ourselves enmeshed in that awful and terrible conflict. Well, to a man, just like that, that terrible war swept those men off of their feet. They were just lost and confused. The greatest preacher of their kind quit preaching. He just quit his pulpit and gave it over to somebody else.

But we are not that way. Not us! We have already been told that much tribulation lies ahead. Blood lies ahead. There lies ahead the great day of the wrath and judgment of almighty God. These days in the past are just patterns, they are just types, they are just pictures of the great and final Armageddon. When those awful days come and tragedy strikes, you are not of the night, as if that day should take you unaware and surprised. God's Word says, as long as there is a tooth that can be bared to bite, as long as there is a fist that can be doubled to fight, as long as there is the beast and the ape and the tiger in humanity, it will be the same story of blood and war and destruction.

We believers can more accurately evaluate what goes on in, say, the Kremlin today. We are not really expecting peace, and we are not really expecting to dwell each under his own vine and his own fig tree. We don't expect communism to be successful; we don't expect capitalism to be successful. We are not all going to have two Cadillacs in every garage and live in forty-room mansions. We realize fully that peace and safety is not our lot in life. But to unconverted men, the manifestations of the depths of depravity and the fountains of iniquity that repeatedly pour from our fallen race will come as a complete surprise.

Somehow they continue to trust, and they continue to lose. As long as Satan is out of the pit, and as long as he rules in this earth, his implements are darkness and blood and horror and death.

We are not of the night as if that day should overtake us unaware. Actually, as we observe the machinations of our enemies and as we look with apprehension at the world of men today, we realize that our redemption comes nearer. When these things come to pass, said Jesus, look up! Lift up your heads, for your redemption draweth nigh. It will not be long. For the elect's sake, those days are shortened.

The things that are written in the books of prophecy, such as the passage we are studying now, are certainly not just so much poetry or symbolism, written for our diversion or curiosity. Neither are they written to scare us, for believers ought not to scare easily. No, these great revelations are made so that we might be pilgrims of God. Our Bible is an honest, straightforward, perfectly accurate book of history and prophecy for our admonition, that we might be all the better servants of Jesus.

Paul gives appeals that we not sleep as others do, but that we watch and be sober; for they that sleep, sleep in the night, and they that be drunken are drunken in the night. In view of the great and final coming of the Lord and the denouement of this age, let us not be drunken with anything. The glamour and pleasures and enticements of the world are there, but let us not be drunken. Let us not sleep as they do in the night. Let us be sober, looking up to God.

Let us who are of the day be sober, putting on the breastplate of faith and hope and love. These are the graces that God has bestowed upon us.

"God hath not appointed us to wrath, but to obtain salvation by our Lord Jesus Christ, who died for us, that whether we wake or sleep, we should live together with him" (1 Thess. 5:9). You do not have anything to be afraid of; not you, not us.

When I was a little boy, I had a terrible dream. I dreamed the great last day had come, and the whole world was before the judgment seat of God, and I was there, and I was lost. And I was being sent away into eternal perdition and damnation. I was just a little fellow, after all. I awoke and was crying in fear, and I ran to my mother and daddy in their bedroom. Mother said, "Why, Son?" And she said, "Come, my son." As I lay down by her, she quieted me and soon after that I found the Lord. Now, I do not ever need to be afraid—never.

Jesus died for us that whether we wake, that is whether we are alive at his coming and are translated, or whether we sleep, whether our bodies are buried in the earth, we should live together with him. All the wrath and judgment of God, the "day of the Lord" and the tribulation, will never touch God's people. They will be protected with the Lord. He will take to himself his own, and that precedes it all.

Paul concludes his appeals: "Wherefore comfort yourselves together and edify one another, even as also ye do" (v. 11). Lift up your heart, my brother. Lift up your faith, my sister. Be of good courage, my yokefellow. It is all in God's hands. And if the storm comes, he rides above it. And if death comes, and oh, how it comes, he is the Lord of life. Whether we wake, whether we are here, or whether we sleep, if we fall before he comes, we shall still live together with him.

All of it—the prophecies, the coming destruction, the suddenness of it all—means just this: If we have Jesus, we have a hope, a destiny, a life, a day, a glory. And if we do not have Jesus, we are lost. It is nothing but the night and the dark and the doom.

We wonder, under these circumstances, how a man could say I would rather die, I would rather be lost, I would rather be in hell, I would rather be damned, I would rather spend eternity in suffering and agony, I would rather be shut out with the door closed. I would rather be sent away. I would rather be lost than to open my heart to the saving grace of Jesus and have my name written in the Lamb's Book of Life. Could a man ever utter all that? No, not if he knew God's Word.

Let us be the good servants we are admonished to be. Let us make the choice clear. Let us tell our friends, our neighbors, all men what we have seen in the prophecy of the Bible. Let us go to those who perceive the siren and yet ignore it, and make the alternative clear. Let us take to them the most precious hope that we have, the hope in Jesus.

8
The Great Separation

There is to be a great separation in times to come in the human race.

When the Lord comes for the believers, when the church is translated to heaven, many will be left behind; and that is very clear from the scriptures. There will never be a clearer distinction between believer and unbeliever than in that day when God places them virtually in different worlds.

Paul describes the rapture of the church in marvelously powerful words in 1 Thessalonians 4:14-18: "For if we believe that Jesus died and rose again, even so them also which sleep in Jesus will God bring with him. For this we say unto you by the word of the Lord, that we which are alive and remain unto the coming of the Lord shall not prevent [precede] them which are asleep. For the Lord himself shall descend from heaven with a shout, with the voice of the archangel, and with the trump of God: and the dead in Christ shall rise first: Then we who are alive and remain shall be caught up together with them in the clouds, to meet the Lord in the air: and so shall we ever be with the Lord. Wherefore comfort one another with these words."

We should note again that those who died in Christ, "them which are asleep," will also be raised, and in fact they will be the first raised. Then we who are alive and remain will join them in the clouds to meet the Lord in the air. This passage obviously confronts life and death and gives them new meaning. Believers, those who died and those who are alive, form one group—the group to be separated and taken to heaven. Unbelievers, dead and alive, remain.

We can notice that throughout the Bible what is spoken of as life, and for comfort, invariably has in it words concerning death and damnation. The two go together in God's writing, and there is no escaping that relationship. Paul wrote in 2 Corinthians 2, "For we are unto God a sweet savour of Christ, in them that are saved, and in them that perish: To the one we are the savour of death unto death; and to the other the savour of life unto life" (v. 16). The same gospel message that saves some shall also condemn others (who refuse it or repudiate it). That pillar of fire by night and the cloud by day was a strength and a help and a sign of the presence of Jehovah to his people. But to the Egyptians it was dark and foreboding and spoke of judgment, death, and damnation.

In verse 18 we are told: "Wherefore, comfort one another with these words." And they are surely a comfort to those who have lost a believing loved one. Our dead in Christ shall rise first. They shall see the Lord; they shall be clothed in his likeness and filled with his fullness. And we who are alive and remain at that coming shall be caught up with them to meet our Lord in the air. In a moment, in the twinkling of an eye, we shall be immortalized, glorified, transfigured. All of God's sainted dead and all of God's sainted and forgiven and justified believers in Christ shall be taken out of the world and shall meet the Lord in the air.

Well may we comfort one another with these words.

But consider for a moment: what is comfort to us, hope for us, life and light and glory for us, amounts to damnation for those who will abide and remain. There certainly will be a great separation when the earth is left without a Christian.

All of God's people will be taken away from the world. Of that event our Lord spoke most solemnly.

We find that great coming separation depicted as the theme throughout the whole revelation of the word of God. For example, in the Sermon on the Mount our Lord said, "Not every one that saith unto me, Lord, Lord, shall enter the kingdom of heaven. . . . Many will say to me in that day, Lord, Lord, have we not prophesied in thy name? [False preachers, filling the pulpits!] and in thy name have cast out devils? [They say they work miracles in his name.] and in thy name done many wonderful works? And then will I profess unto them, I never knew you: depart from me, ye that work iniquity" (Matt. 7:21-23). There is the separation.

Another example from the lips of our Savior is in the parabolic chapter, Matthew 13: "The kingdom of heaven is like unto a net, that was cast into the sea, and gathered every kind: Which, when it was full, they drew to shore . . . and gathered the good into vessels, but cast the bad away. So shall it be at the end of the world: the angels shall come forth, and sever the wicked from among the just, and shall cast them into the furnace of fire: there shall be wailing and gnashing of teeth" (vv. 47-50). The great separation again.

And then again from the lips of the Lord in Luke 13: "Strive to enter in at the strait gate: for many, I say unto you, will seek to enter in, and shall not be able. When once the master of the house is risen up, and hath shut the door, and ye begin to stand without, and to knock at the door, saying, Lord, Lord, open unto us: and he shall answer and say unto you, I know you not whence ye are: Then shall ye begin to say, We have eaten and drunk in thy presence, and thou hast taught in our streets. But he shall say, I tell you, I know you not whence ye are: depart from me" (vv. 24-27).

And again in Luke 17 the Lord says, "I tell you, in that night there shall be two men in one bed; the one shall be taken, and the other shall be left. Two women shall be grinding together; the one shall be taken and the other left. Two men shall be in the field; the one shall be taken, and the other left" (vv. 34-36).

Many kinds of men profess their faith in the Lord Jesus Christ. This is the church age, the age of grace, when we all have an opportunity to believe in Jesus. But there are professors of faith in Christ who give every evidence of being real and genuine and acceptable to God, and there are professors of faith in the name of Christ who give *no* evidence of being acceptable to God. Some who preach Christ give no evidence whatever of being genuinely saved or converted.

Well, there is a time coming when God shall separate these two. Those who are not real, who have not been saved, who are not regenerated, will be left behind in the world. We mortal men are not always able to draw these fine distinctions; but when God makes the judgment, there will indeed be a great separation.

When Grace Abounds

The door leading to the kingdom of God and into heaven has been left ajar for us in this age. Paul says this dispensation of grace, this *oikonomia* (it could be translated "administration"), represents an era in which God deals with the human race in a certain covenant way.

In the Bible we have an old covenant and a new covenant, an old dispensation and a new dispensation, two kinds of contracts as it were.

When we look at the old covenant, we see a variety of ways that God has wrought with men. God walked with man in the Garden of Eden in the days and age of innocence; he worked in certain ways before the flood in the antediluvian age; he dealt with men differently in the days of the patriarchs and of the Mosaic covenant. God has chosen to operate different "administrations" in his dealings with men.

We are in our own peculiar dispensation now, our age of grace. We have this unprecedented opportunity for the salvation of all men, for the preaching of the gospel of the saving Son of God.

Then going beyond us there is to be another age, an *oikonomia*, a dispensation in a millennial kingdom when we shall see God visibly and the kingdom shall have come. Then beyond that, the ages of the ages, the eternity of the eternities. The millennial kingdom ends when Satan is loosed for a season. The great white throne judgment, which is the judgment of the wicked dead, follows, and finally we come to the renovated heavens and earth and the New Jerusalem, the city of God where we are forever with the Lord.

Now our present age, this day, this hour in which we live represents a certain set period of time known to God. As it began at a certain time it shall end at a certain time. We men do not know the times and seasons of the Father—we do not know the length of this age—but God has revealed to us how this age began and how it will close.

This day of grace, this day of the church, this day of the Holy Spirit, began secretly, quietly. This day of the opportunity of the preaching of the gospel, this day when

we can be saved by looking to Jesus began secretly in
the womb of a virgin named Mary. It began in the quiet
resurrection of our Lord and his breathing upon the disciples: "Receive ye the breath, the spirit, the *pneuma* of
God." Then it began openly and publicly at the festival
of Pentecost, where men of every nation under the sun
heard the saving announcement of the gospel of the Son
of God in their own mother language. Every man understood the Savior that great day as plainly as he understood
his own native tongue.

I believe that the scripture teaches that it shall end in
that same way. This day of grace, this day of the church,
this day of opportunity to trust in Jesus shall end first
secretly, quietly, like the stealth of a thief. The coming
of the Lord for his saints will be any day, any moment,
any time, any hour. We shall be caught up to be with
the Lord in the air. And then it shall end openly and
publicly, like the vivid lightning across the bosom of the
sky. The Lord shall come visibly, openly, triumphantly
to be glorified with his saints.

This in-between time—this pause between the coming
of the Spirit and the rapture of believers—is our day of
grace.

A Day of Salvation

There are those who accept the Lord in his proffered
mercies. There are those who believe in Jesus, and they
give every evidence of being really saved and acceptable
unto God.

Anybody can say, "I do not believe." Anybody can
refuse. It takes no learning, it takes no commitment. It
takes no scholarship, it takes no praying, it takes no godli-
ness. It takes no repentance, it takes nothing at all to be
an unbeliever. It is our natural state, after all.

But to believe, to accept Jesus as Savior, is to have the seal of the elective call and purpose of God.

The true children of God open their hearts to the appeal of the Spirit. They openly, publicly, gladly announce their faith in the Lord Jesus. They stand and confess him with their mouths. Faith comes by hearing, and hearing the Word of God.

Real Christians love the Word of God, the written Word and the Incarnate Word, our Savior in heaven—and the spoken, preached word as the Lord's servants stand to proclaim the mercies and love of God.

Real Christians love the house of the Lord. We are glad when our neighbor paraphrases the Scriptures, "Let us go up to the house of the Lord. Our feet shall stand within its gates." They love the fellowship and the communion of the saints. These are the people of Christ. These are of our own family; these are our brothers and our sisters.

And true believers love the lost. They create missions to take the saving word of Christ to sinners. They reach the lost across the sea, in our own homeland, and among those everywhere whose souls are in doubt and jeopardy. When an appeal is made and some come to Christ, there is joy in the soul of a real, genuine, converted Christian, and there is gladness in his heart. I have seen godly men and women with the tears falling unashamedly from their faces, just looking upon the sight of men and women coming to Christ. Just the sight of it and the knowledge of the meaning of it, the washing away of sins in the Blood of the Lamb, the writing of the name in the Book of Life, and the hope we have in heaven, moves the soul of the child of God.

But there is another profession of faith that gives no evidence of being true and genuine and acceptable to God, none at all. These "believers" may be religious, but they

are not spiritual. To them churches are places to marry
the young and to bury the dead. If they attend the services,
it is a matter of appearing respectable. In every congregation there are those whose names are on the church roll
who give no evidence of being born again.

I remember a fine man and his wife who came to our
city from another great city. He was an officer in his church
there, came to Dallas, and now in affluence and in pros-
perity he moves in a glittering circle. But wealth and success
have turned his head, and in pride he passes by his church,
and he passes by his Lord, and he passes by the work
of the kingdom of Christ. I don't understand how he could
neglect Christ if he were truly a saved man.

I have never been able to understand how a man could
say, "I can't love God anymore and don't want to," just
because he became rich. The only explanation I can give
for it is just this: when a man is not really saved, when
he is not really genuine, whether he is poor or whether
he is rich the fortunes of life will take him away like the
wind blows the chaff. But if a man is really saved, if he
is regenerated, if he loves God, if there is a new heart
and a new life and peace in his soul, whether he had a
billion times a billion dollars or whether he languished
in hunger and thirst, it would be just the same. Living
with the Lord, in infirmity with the Lord; in poverty with
the Lord, in affluence with the Lord; whether to live or
to die, whether to be there or here; a big house or a little
one; known or unknown; still and all, forever with the
Lord.

The coming great separation is God's business. As for
now, the tares and the wheat are to grow side by side.
It is not for us to do the separating. That is the prerogative
of heaven; that belongs to the omnipotent God. Men are
to be left to their own choices, side by side, the tares and

the wheat, the good and the bad together in the net, the two working in the field, the two sleeping in the bed, the two grinding at the mill, side by side.

But someday, some imminent day, a day known only to God, there shall be that moment, that instant, that twinkling of an eye. There shall be the catching away, the lifting up to heaven of God's people. There shall be the rapture, the translation, the immortalization of God's beloved in this earth who have placed their trust in him. They that are dead, resurrected to a life of glory; they who have remained, translated in a moment, in a second, in the twinkling of an eye.

And at that moment of the great separation all of the unregenerate, all of the false prophets, false teachers, false systems of Christianity, false preachers of the gospel, unbelievers, the world of darkness and death and blasphemy will be left behind. And the world will be without a Christian.

Obviously, that day will be awful for some. Jesus tells us with his supernatural insight: "As it was in the days of Noe, so shall it be also in the days of the Son of man. They did eat, they drank, they married wives, they were given in marriage, until the day that Noe entered into the ark and the flood came, and destroyed them all" (Luke 17:26-27). Our Lord's image is clear. When Noah and his family entered the ark and God shut the door, there was not a living righteous man in the earth. Outside that door, blasphemy and iniquity and hypocrisy, and the unregenerate and the darkness of judgment remained. The great separation! Not a righteous man, not a justified man, not a saved man, not a forgiven man in the earth. All were taken away when God shut the door. Think of this earth without a Christian, without a believing witness, as it was in the days of Noah.

There shall come a night
   of such wild afright
as none besides shall know,
   when the heavens shake
and the wide earth quake
   in her last and deepest woe.
Oh lost one give ear
   while the saints are near.
Soon must the tie be riven
   and men side by side
shall God's hand divide
   as far as hell's depths are from heaven.
Some husband whose head
   was laid in his bed,
throbbing with mad excess
   shall awake from his dream
by the lightning's gleam
   alone in his last distress.
For the patient wife
   who through each day's life
watched and wept for his soul
   is taken away
and no more shall pray
   for the judgments themselves do roll.
The children of day
   summoned away,
left are the children of night,
   sealed in their doom,
there's no more room,
   filled are the mansions of light.

AUTHOR UNKNOWN

A Day of Judgment

Will it change the earth much to be left without a Christian? How will the world get along without us?

Well, the Bible is very clear on that. The Scriptures call that time the great tribulation. The Bible calls it the distress of nations. The Bible calls it the time of Jacob's trouble. Oh, the darkness of those days. Jesus prayed that you may escape from the tribulation of those days when the earth is without a Christian.

Jesus knew men's hearts, and he prayed for their escape from that great tribulation. Anytime one is persuaded that the human race left to itself can work out its own problems and troubles by science and philosophy, and speculation, all he has to do is honestly look at this world when God's hand is withdrawn and God's people are taken away. It will be a world of unmitigated blasphemy and iniquity, and unprecedented violence and bloodshed. As it was in the terrifying days of Noah, so shall it be in those terrible days. Nations shall arm themselves in all parts of the globe, and they will lift terrible swords against each other. And in the picture in Revelation the four horsemen of the apocalypse shall ride as they always do, but now more definitely: The white horseman conquering, the red horseman indicating war and blood, the black horseman of starvation and famine, and the fourth horseman bringing violent death, when the world is without a Christian. The judgment of God will be poured out like vials of wrath.

Dear God, who is able for these things? Our refuge is found only in Christ. Our hope is in him. Lord, which of us is able in the little lives that we live and the inevitable death that we face to contemplate such terror? We need the Savior. We need him in that day of judgment, that hour of need. We need him as our advocate before the judgment of God.

That is finally and ultimately what it is to be a Christian—to lean upon Jesus, to depend completely on him. The Son of God will surely present us without fault or blemish to God in that great and final hour. The prayer of every converted child of God is the prayer of the thief dying on the cross beside Jesus: "Lord, remember me when thou comest into thy kingdom" (Luke 23:42).

9
Knowing the Times

"The Pharisees also with the Sadducees came, and tempting desired him that he would shew them a sign from heaven.

He answered and said unto them, When it is evening, ye say, It will be fair weather: for the sky is red.

And in the morning, It will be foul weather to day: for the sky is red and lowering. O ye hypocrites, ye can discern the face of the sky; but can ye not discern the signs of the times?" (Matt. 16:1-3).

"And that, knowing the time, that now it is high time to awake out of sleep: for now is our salvation nearer than when we believed.

The night is far spent, the day is at hand: let us therefore cast off the works of darkness, and let us put on the armour of light.

Let us walk honestly, as in the day; not in rioting and drunkenness, not in chambering and wantonness, not in strife and envying.

But put ye on the Lord Jesus Christ, and make not provision for the flesh, to fulfil the lusts thereof" (Rom. 13:11-14).

God's preacher is to stand before God's people and

proclaim God's message, hopefully with power. He takes God's holy revelation and applies it to his own generation, and to the congregation among whom God has raised him up to be a minister and prophet of the Word.

The Bible contains many prophecies; they are found from the beginning to the end of it. Time and time again you have a prophetic "speaking forth," not only in the sense of exhortation (addressing God's Word to the will of a man, calling on him to give his life to God and to follow the will of God), but you also have many, many prophecies in the sense of an unveiling (an *apokalupsis*) of what is to happen. Paul makes an appeal in the passage quoted above for us to "walk honestly, as in the day; not in rioting and drunkenness, not in chambering and wantonness, not in strife and envy," because knowing the time, it is high time to awake out of our sleep and indifference; for now is our salvation nearer than when we believed. "The night is far spent, the day is at hand."

What kind of a "day" is that to which Paul refers? "The night is far spent, the day is at hand." Is that to be a day of the great judgment of God? Is it to be a day of the great appearing of the Lord? Or is it to be a day of the conversion of the world to Christ? Is it to be a day of peace, a day of universal joy and pleasure and gladness? What kind of a day is that? I have studied many messages and interpretations concerning that day. Out of those addresses I have taken some typical explanations given as the men preach to their people about the future of this world and what lies ahead.

What Men Have Said Concerning a Final Day

First, there was a preacher named Heartpence who was pastor of the First Presbyterian Church in Nashville, Tennessee. I have a copy of a sermon that he preached on this subject. Now listen to this illustrious and scholarly divine as he preached at the end of 1858:

The night of earth's mental and moral darkness is certainly passing away. The morning star is in the morrow sky. Since man's creation, a night of 5,860 years [he has really figured it down to a fine point] has rolled away. Not till the present century could Zion's watchmen see that the night is far spent. Glance at the signs of progress. During the last fifty years, what has been done for man's material and temporal interest! What progress in science and art! What expansion and increase in wealth and commerce! How steam and electricity minister to human want and happiness! What facilities for trade and travel! As the night rolls on, we see uncommon tendencies to a general amelioration of man's condition. The faith of all Christendom is going to work. Ignorance and despotism are waning. The cross makes the crescent give way before the march of a spiritual and purer Christianity. [That is what he said, but at this very moment, for every one convert we make in Africa, the Muslim makes ten.] What hath God wrought even in the past year? Some of the most memorable events in the world's history ever recorded happened in 1858. In view of them, the church can almost anticipate the song of final triumph. Hallelujah! Salvation and glory and honor and power to the Lord our God! The great events of the years seem to converge upon one grand object: the overthrow of idolatry and unbelief, and the rapid spread of a pure Christianity over the globe.

The rebellion in the British Isles . . . [You look at this. The rebellion in the British Isles! What was that rebellion? It was the attempt of a colonial, oppressed people to throw off the yoke of a foreign dictator and to rise to their own national independence. Now look at what he says!] The rebellion in the British Isles, bursting like a storm over that vast empire, threatening to destroy English sway there, has been subdued, and treaties establishing British rule more firmly in Asia and China have sent a paean of praise and thanksgiving throughout the civilized world.

> "Oh, China too is coming
> God's mercies to adore,
> And beauteous isles are shouting,
> Jesus, forevermore."

Hallelujah for the British Empire and for the overthrow of

the independence movement in India; the kingdom of God is
at hand! Look at electricity and look at steam and look at all
of the gadgets God has given us. The millennium is almost here
in 1858.

Before I go on to the next period, may I illustrate how
common that kind of a viewpoint was in those days. Nobel,
the great Swedish inventor, died in 1896. Nobel once said,
"There will never again be war. Absolutely," he said, "by
this invention of dynamite I have made war so terrible
and so awful that men will never fight again. Mankind
will be too afraid of a weapon of such awful destruc-
tiveness." That is what Nobel said, and he gave his Nobel
Peace Prize in honor and memory of the destructive power
of dynamite, thinking that we would never have war anymore. That was in 1896.

The reference to dynamite reminds me of a prophecy
concerning atomic power. Somebody once predicted that
if scientists ever discovered atomic fission and were able
to make nuclear material react to a man's word, the first
use of atomic fission would be in an atomic bomb. That
was said a long time ago. Did the prophecy come true?
Ask Japan and the surviving people of Hiroshima and
Nagasaki.

Let us now come to another period. I am quoting from
the official book of proceedings of the Baptist World Alli-
ance, Second Congress, meeting at Philadelphia, June 19-
25, 1911. Dr. John Clifford, the illustrious Baptist minister
of London, England, was the president. At that great congress they elected Robert Stuart MacArthur, pastor of the
Calvary Baptist Church of New York City, as the new
president. They met in the Grace Baptist Temple in Philadelphia, Dr. Russell H. Conwell's church. Dr. Conwell was
the pastor who authored the famous lecture on "Acres of
Diamonds." Oh, with what optimism and triumphant con-

fidence did they face the future! Surely, the millennium was at hand! Dr. Conwell said in his welcoming address to the Baptist World Congress:

> We have our dear brethren here from Russia. God bless them every one; . . . Let us say to the people of Russia . . . that these brethren are sent back from this great convention with the prayer that they may have Christ going with them everywhere to influence mankind for good . . .

And Dr. Clifford from London, speaking in reply to a comment by our great Baptist theologian, Dr. Augustus Strong, said:

> You have referred, Dr. Strong, to my friend of twenty years, David Lloyd-George [then Prime Minister of the British Empire] . . . Lloyd-George is a working Baptist, and God has raised him up a prophet statesman. . . . Is not our outlook bright? . . . You [in America] have . . . your great tasks given you of God and you are ready surely in the spirit of Christ . . . to set yourselves to those tasks, assured that . . . you will do your utmost so that the kingdom of our God may come all over the world and the freedom we possess today shall be everybody's possession, and the justice which rules in our lands shall rule in all the lands, and so the kingdoms of this world become the kingdoms of our God and of his Christ.

Now I quote from Reverend J. G. Lehmann of Germany. He mentions the close connection between American Baptists and German Baptists. The founder of the German Baptist work, J. G. Oncken, had prayed for years that God would send a man who would baptize him; God answered that prayer by a man from America. Said the Reverend J. G. Lehmann;

> I wish this man Oncken . . . could be present. Perhaps he is . . . perhaps he can hear the report not only from Germany but also from Bohemia and Bulgaria and Denmark and Estonia and Finland and Holland and Lithuania and Moravia and Poland

and Russia and Roumania. For this pioneer has been the means of spreading the gospel and the principles for which Baptists stand . . . through all these countries; and it is a marvel in my eyes and of those of my German brethren here to find what God has done through his mighty power and blessing. From those little cities the blessings have flowed all over Europe.

Remember, this was being said in 1911. Today Lithuania and Estonia have fallen prey to Communism. So have most of the other nations named.

A. U. Kawaguchi of Japan said:

A few days ago the Japanese Minister at Washington said that there had been wars of the roses, but pointing to the stars and stripes of America and the sun flag of Japan he said that there never had been war between the stars and the sun. There will not be war between the sun flag and all the flags of the nations represented here.

. . . Japan, the country which has astonished the world because of her recent progress, . . . is the country where civil and religious liberty reigns . . . Japan is thrown open for evangelism. Go wherever you will and you will find men and women willing to listen to the gospel of our Lord Jesus Christ. . . . May Christ become the King and Lord of Japan.

And finally I quote from W. E. Hatcher who wrote the famous biography of John Jasper. He pastored the Second Baptist Church of Richmond, Virginia. The last sentences of his glorious address were:

I want to say that the Baptists of the South are together. I want to say that the white and colored Baptists work under different organizations but they get along better with each other than either party gets along with itself, and we are working together in full confidence in the conquest of this world for Christ.

They said all of that in 1911. What if some modern Amos had stood up at that World Congress in 1911 and had said, "Three years from now the world will be plunged into the bloodiest war it has ever known; and in 1923 Europe and later the United States will be plunged into the most degrading depression it has ever known; and in 1939 with the invasion of Poland the world will a second time be plunged into the most frightful and terrible war in recorded history; and five years after the end of the second global war Korea will be a bloody battlefield for America; and the nation of the Orient called China will bring nuclear terror to the free world, trepidation, and trembling of heart because of the possibility of complete annihilation from their hydrogen hell bombs; and on into the last quarter of the twentieth century there will continue to be bloody conflict in Southeast Asia supported by the Communist nations of Russia and China"?

Had a modern Amos stood up in 1911 and said that, they would have said to him: "Back to your sheep! Back to your sycamore trees! Back to the wilderness of Judea! We are the harbingers of the glorious millennium, the conquest of the world for Christ!"

I have heard this theological point of view all my life. Never was I taught any other thing, never! My old New Testament teacher was Dr. A. T. Robertson, the greatest Greek scholar Southern Baptists ever produced, and perhaps the greatest our modern world has ever known. I studied under him four years. He was an illustrious professor and a wonderful man. I quote from the preface of his book, *The New Citizenship*, written in 1919:

> The present book is the reaction of the author's own mind to the new situation. . . . Victory has crowned the army of America and her allies. The new day has dawned for which we toiled and prayed. World peace has come . . . the task before us now is to apply the energy and organization to the destruction of foes in the home camp . . . King Alcohol has been dethroned [we had just passed the eighteenth amendment]. . . . The reign of the politician with his graft and his greed is over.

What God Has Revealed

My brothers and sisters in Jesus, I could quote things like that to you by the day and the hour and the year. So what is the matter with these men? Were they not holy men and devout? Were they not prayerful men? Did they not love God? Did they not try to preach his truths? Yes sir! Some of these men I have known personally, like my old teacher. They were unquestionably devout and holy men. Well, what was the matter with them? There is just one thing the matter with them, and it is this. When a man reads the Bible, he may read it with preconceived notions. When he does that he may so twist its message and so turn its meaning until he practically refuses to let the Bible speak for itself. I may also be unconsciously affected by preconceptions, but I do know that nobody in this world ever taught me the interpretation of the consummation of the age that I think I see here in the Bible. I was never taught it in my life. I just started out preaching the Bible, and here are some things I found there.

Daniel says: "the end thereof shall be with a flood, and unto the end of the war desolations are determined." Here is an actual Hebrew translation of Daniel 9:26: "And unto the end war is determined." God wrote that in his Book. Look again in Matthew 24 where Jesus says nation shall rise against nation, kingdom against kingdom. There shall be famines and pestilences, and all of these are the beginning of sorrows. And he thus speaks on and on and on. In Revelation 16 John writes:

"And I saw three unclean spirits like frogs come out of the mouth of the dragon, and out of the mouth of the beast, and out of the mouth of the false prophet.

For they are the spirits of devils, working miracles, which go forth unto the kings of the earth and of the whole world, to gather them to the battle of that great day of God Almighty.

Behold, I come as a thief. Blessed is he that watcheth, and keepeth his garments, lest he walk naked, and they see his shame.

And he gathered them together into a place called in the Hebrew tongue Armageddon" (vv. 13-16).

You may talk about evolving into peace and bringing in the millennium and preaching the world into universal conversion, but God's Book says the end of this age will be when the rulers of the earth shall be gathered together in a battle called the battle of Armageddon. Turn over to Revelation 19, and you find the angel calling the beasts and vultures and creeping things to eat the flesh of the captains and the great men, because of their destruction in their war against him that sat on the throne and against his army (vv. 17-18). And in Revelation 20, after the millennium, "when the thousand years are expired, Satan shall be loosed out of his prison, and shall go out to deceive the nations which are in the four quarters of the earth, Gog and Magog, to gather them together to battle: the number of whom is as the sand of the sea" (vv. 7-8). That is the closing scene in the history of the earth. Fire comes down from God and destroys the enemies of Christ. Following that holocaust we are introduced to the great white throne judgment of the wicked dead. From the beginning of this Book to the end, it says what lies ahead is tribulation, suffering, war, and battle. Men's hearts will be fainting within them for fear of what is to come. That is what the Book says. How does that compare with what man says?

The Illusion of Progress

Let me discuss for a moment the reason why I think men have erroneous preconceptions concerning a manmade reign of peace in a manmade Eden. I think that men say these things because of the illusion of progress. For example, if one visits the Smithsonian Institution he will see the way people rode in an oxcart, then in a covered wagon, next in a rubber-tired buggy with a two-cylinder engine. Here is the way men rode when Ford made his T-model, and there is the way people rode when he came out with his A-model. Over here is the way we ride today: automatic transmission, power steering, power brakes, radial tires, air conditioning. Look at the progress made in travel. There is even the jet airplane. Look at us! The progress we are making! The kingdom of God is at hand!

In the Smithsonian Institution one can also trace the history of communications. In ancient days they used to send a message by writing notes on rocks. That can be illustrated by the ancient cuneiform inscriptions. Then they had papyri, next parchment, then the printing press. More recently the radio was invented, then television. Just look at the progress we are making in communications. The kingdom of God is at hand!

Or take the matter of luxuries. In the ancient times, in the days of the Roman noblemen, swift runners came out of the snow-capped Alps bearing ice and snow down to the noblemen's wine tables for a banquet in the city of Rome. They drank wine cooled by the snow of the Alps, brought by the panting runners. A long time ago a beautiful lady such as a queen would be carried through the streets of an ancient city in a sedan chair borne on the shoulders of four slaves, each one standing at a corner. Compare the luxuries of today. Look at the refrigerator. Look at our bakeries. Look at our clothing shops. (We do not have to sew anymore.) We hardly have to do anything anymore. Look at all of these marvelous luxuries we have. The kingdom of God has come! But has it?

Surely, surely it is an illusion—this so-called progress. Have we really progressed?

We can travel better, yes, but are we going better places? We can see better, yes, but are we seeing better things? We can hear better, yes, but are we hearing nobler words? Are we producing men today like Abraham, Isaiah, Peter, John, and Paul? We are surely producing in modern times earthshaking and famous men: Hitler, Stalin, Tojo, the bloody dictators of Asia, Africa, South America, and even figures of Watergate in America. Progress? Are you sure? In the book *Thinking Black*, the missionary Dan Crawford is telling a big black man all of the things he would find in modern civilization. The big fellow, unimpressed, folded his arms and said, "But sir, to be better off is not to be better."

Our glorious cities of today can point to magnificent sculptured pieces and to beautiful paintings and to marvelous buildings, but what do you do about the sculptor and the painter and the builder? He is still as sinful and wicked and unconverted as he ever was. Progress? Are you sure?

Our Basis for Hope

There is progress and development in all history—that is right. There is progress from immaturity to maturity in all history—that is right. But do not forget while you are progressing, making a better automobile, making a better refrigerator, making a better television set, making a better gadget, you are also progressing in aerial bombing; you are also progressing in the ability to disseminate political lies and propaganda over radio and television to deceive half of the total population of the world and to give it an illusion instead of the truth. While we invent better gadgets, we also progress in iniquity and in evil and in murder and in blood and in the ability to destroy.

My conclusion is thus firmly avowed: there is not a vestigial remnant of evidence to be found in all history that good ever overtakes evil. It is like a cycle that is vicious and terrible. The world was evil in the days of Abraham; it was evil in the days of Isaiah; it was evil in the days of Jesus; it was evil in the days of Paul. It was evil in the days of Charlemagne; it was evil in the days of Napoleon Bonaparte; it was evil in the days of Isabella II; it was evil in the days of Hitler and Tojo and Mussolini. And it is evil today. If things continue to go as they have in these days past, I can see no other thing than that the hour will inevitably come when the whole world will become another Hiroshima, wailing, trembling before the lurid death that falls out of the sky. There has never been a people that hesitated or refused to use their most destructive weapons to achieve their ultimate gain. Countries have used gunpowder, dynamite, the atomic bomb, and one day the hydrogen bomb or whatever can be developed beyond that will be used, even though it will mean the dissolution of civilization and the annihilation of mankind. Not in history is there any measurable hope on the part of the "goodness" of man to achieve an ultimate triumph for the peace and glory and salvation of the world.

"My God and my soul, pastor," you cry. "Then we face death, we face annihilation, we face want and destruction. O preacher, what a terrible gospel, what a despair!" Ah, no! I have a Book in my hand. In that Book I read where Paul said: "Knowing the time . . . for now is our salvation nearer than when we believed. The night is far spent, the day is at hand" (Rom. 13:11-12). What did he mean? He meant the same thing the Lord Jesus meant when he said:

"And there shall be signs in the sun, and in the moon, and in the stars; and upon the earth distress of nations, with perplexity; the sea and the waves roaring;
Men's hearts failing them for fear, and for looking after those things which are coming on the earth: for the powers of heaven shall be shaken.
And then shall they see the Son of man coming in a cloud with power and great glory.
And when these things begin to come to pass, then look up, and lift up your heads; for your redemption draweth nigh" (Luke 21:25-28).

And then shall we sing in all truth: "Blessing, and honour, and glory, and power, be unto him that sitteth upon the throne, and unto the Lamb for ever and ever and ever" (Rev. 5:13). And like the twenty-four elders, we will bow down and worship him who is King and Lord of all the nations and people of the earth. (See Rev. 5:14.)

I am not discouraged. You cannot discourage me. I am not downhearted. They cannot get me to be downhearted. And I am not in despair. Why? Because the Lord God Omnipotent reigns. When death and destruction and tribulation overwhelm our earth like a flood, there is, then comes, and here reigns our Lord and our King, Christ Jesus. He is coming in the glory of the clouds bringing with him those who have loved and adored him in this earth; and that is what we are to be doing until he comes, showing our love and adoration for him by keeping his commandments. Let us cast off the works of darkness, and put on the armor of light. Let us walk honestly, as in the day, and put on the Lord Jesus Christ, "for the day is at hand."

10
The Signs of
His Coming

"And as he sat upon the mount of Olives, the disciples came unto him privately, saying, Tell us, when shall these things be? and what shall be the sign of thy coming, and of the end of the world?" (Matt. 24:3).

The Bible abounds with signs which will reveal to the spiritual Christian the imminency of the second coming of Christ. If we ignore these signs, we become like the people in Jesus' day who were rebuked and castigated for not knowing the signs of his first coming (Matt. 16:2-3). The Jewish nation rejected Jesus as their Messiah because it did not believe their prophets spoke literally concerning a suffering Savior. The people were too caught up in the busy affairs of the day, and in their all-consuming passion to find a leader to champion a rebellion against Rome, to sense and to see what God was doing in sending them their great Redeemer. Not knowing the prophets, not searching the Scriptures, they missed him completely. Shall we do the same? God grant that as we watch and wait for his second coming we may believe the Scriptures literally and follow in faith the mighty hand of God as he shapes human history for its rendezvous with the coming King.

Jesus gave us many signs and indications of his coming again, by which we might know that his return is imminent. We are always to live in view of the imminency of the coming of Christ. In speaking of these signs he says, "When ye shall see all these things, know that it is near, even at the door" (Matt. 24:33). Even though we are not to know the day and the hour (Matt. 24:36) we may know the general time when he will come back again. One thing we do know is that we are nearer the coming of Christ today than we have been ever before in all of history. Each day brings us one day closer to this mighty event. We believe that there are things revealed in prophecy that are pressing with rapidity toward fulfillment.

The prophetic revelations of God's program that are unfolded for us are the events of the tribulation period. The Word of God is very specific concerning the dramatic, catastrophic changes that will take place in the earth after the church has been raptured. The translation, or the rapture of the church, is without signs to warn us of its proximity. Yet, there are foreshadowings of events that will come to their consummation after the church is gone. These fore-shadowings are already appearing on the world scene, and because of these things the rapture, which has to precede these specific, prophetic events, could be near. Jesus may come at any moment. Nothing more needs to happen as far as we can find in the Scriptures. The "blessed hope" of the return of the Lord Jesus Christ for his church is what we are waiting for. The coming of the Lord means the release of every believer from the curse and bondage of mortality here on earth, when we rise to meet him in the air and, in glorified, resurrected bodies, serve him forever. The Word of God gives us many lights, but these lights do not herald the translation of the church. The next event in prophecy, the rapture, is a signless and unannounced event, and God has given us no indication as to when it may come. Its nearness may only be known by the character of the times.

Since the rapture is to be at least seven years prior to Christ's second coming to earth, and the signs indicating the nearness of this second coming to earth after the tribulation are already in the process of fulfillment, we can imagine how near the rapture itself must be. The complete fulfillment of the signs in Matthew 24 will occur after the church is translated. If they are already beginning to take place, we may confidently say that the rapture must be nearer than we realize. The entire passage in Matthew 24 and 25 was written to answer this question concerning the sign of the coming of the Messiah which will terminate the age.

The Apocalyptic Discourse of Jesus

In Matthew 23 Jesus had exposed the character of the Jewish ecclesiastics, announcing the judgments of God against them for their unfaithfulness, which was bringing ruin upon the nation. In verses 38 and 39 he sadly predicts the destruction of the Temple and the nation of Israel; also, his own future coming. "Behold, your house is left unto you desolate. For I say unto you, Ye shall not see me henceforth till ye shall say, Blessed is he that cometh in the name of the Lord." In Matthew 24 we read that Jesus departed from the Temple. This ended his public ministry. As he withdrew, the presence of God left the sanctuary and the Temple was given over to destruction:

"And Jesus went out, and departed from the temple: and his disciples came to him for to shew him the buildings of the temple. And Jesus said unto them, See ye not all

these things? verily I say unto you, There shall not be
left here one stone upon another, that shall not be thrown
down" (Matt. 24:1-2).

The destruction of such a magnificent building seemed
impossible to his disciples. The blocks of stones were mas-
sive, some of them nearly twenty-four feet long. In the
minds of the disciples, such a disaster as the destruction
of the Temple could connect only with the last days, so
that is why they asked these questions in Matthew 24:3
regarding the signs of his coming. Probably the promise
of his return in Matthew 23:39 had given the disciples
this eschatological association. Daniel had predicted that
there would be a destruction of Jerusalem and of the
sanctuary (Dan. 9:26). But the prophecies of Daniel and
of Jesus in this Olivet discourse were not completely fulfilled by Titus in A.D. 70, nor have they been completely
fulfilled since. Later on in this discourse, Jesus put all of
these prophecies into the future, connecting them with his
coming in glory. This was difficult for the disciples to
understand. To them Jesus' prediction of the destruction
of the temple, to be followed by the "abomination of
desolation" standing in the temple (Matt. 24:15) must have
seemed like a hopeless contradiction, but if you put a
Temple in Jerusalem, the Olivet discourse will suddenly
become clear, and there *will* be a new Temple built in
Jerusalem before Christ comes again (see 2 Thess. 2:3-4;
Dan. 9:27). *God explains prophecy by fulfilling it.*

Jesus pinpointed the general time of his return as he
answered the question of the disciples, "What will be the
sign of your coming?" and "What will be the sign of the
end of the age?" "The coming" referred to in the question
is the second advent of Christ. It was only natural that

they wanted to know what signs would indicate his return to set up God's promised kingdom. Jesus did not say one word concerning the rapture, but the discourse concerns the judgment upon Jerusalem, the final judgment at the end of the age, and the setting up of the kingdom.

The judgment upon Jerusalem was a type of the coming judgment upon the world. Jesus told them in this Olivet discourse how they might discern the coming destruction of Jerusalem: When they saw the abomination of desolation (the idolatrous Roman standard) standing in the temple, the awesome day was at hand. They were not to delay in departing from the city (Matt. 24:15-21). The tragedy of the Roman conquest of Jerusalem in A.D. 70 is a dramatic picture of the ultimate tribulation. What happened in A.D. 70 is a type of the terrible visitation in the future, and the signal that the great tribulation is about to start will be their sight of "the abomination of desolation" standing in the holy place of their rebuilt Temple. The "abomination of desolation" will be the image of the Antichrist set up in the temple (2 Thess. 2:3-4, Rev. 13:14-15). An "abomination of desolation" was placed in the sanctuary in 165 B.C. when an invading king named Antiochus Epiphanes slaughtered a pig in the holy place. This prophecy of Jesus tells us that the Jews will have to be in possession of their ancient city of Jerusalem at the time of the second advent, and a third Temple will be rebuilt upon its ancient site. According to the law of Moses this place is Mount Moriah, where stands today the Dome of the Rock (The Mosque of Omar). Prophecy demands that this mosque be obliterated. It will be, but only God knows how that will take place.

The believing Jews were to flee for their lives from Palestine in the war of A.D. 66-70 and also at the time of the end (Isa. 26:20-21). Many saints in that day will be called upon to lay down their lives under the reign of the Antichrist. The increase of the violation of God's law among the wicked will test the love of many, but the test of reality is endurance (Matt. 24:13). As the last half of the tribulation comes to a close. Jerusalem will be a putrid carcass, around which the eagles will be gathered (Matt. 24:28).

Matthew 24:27-31 describes the return of the Lord. His coming will be with the brilliance of lightning, and it will be watched by the whole world. Every eye shall see him, and the families and tribes of the earth will wail because of him (Rev. 1:7). The great day of the judgment of almighty God has come.

In this Olivet discourse Jesus gave many general signs involving world conditions. These signs—such as religious apostasy, wars, earthquakes, famines—would increase in frequency and intensity just like birth pangs before a child is born. The Lord also delineated many characteristics of the present church age and then of the tribulation period after rapture. There will be wars and rumors of wars when nation shall rise against nation. But there have always been wars and rumors of wars. Jesus said that, in itself, would not be a sign of the end of the age. In Matthew 24:6, he said, "The end is not connected with that" (KJV reads, "but the end is not yet"). There are weapons today—nuclear, chemical, and biological, besides the intercontinental ballistic missiles—which, when released, would destroy the world, except for divine intervention. There will be famines and pestilences. These go hand in hand (poverty and disease). The problem of food supplies is the major cause of worry in about 90 percent of the nations of the earth. There will be false Christs and false prophets, cults, fads, and counterfeit systems which use the name of Christ, but which have departed from the Word. These are rapidly spreading over the world. Many will come, saying, "I am Christ" (Matt. 24:5,11,23-26). Jesus warns not to follow them. Truth is the only answer to false teaching, but truth is a preventative, not always a cure. Truth needs to get there first. The road into a false religion is usually a one-way street. Not many find their way out of it.

Jesus so plainly says that there will be divisions and conflicts, but he also says that these things are not evidences of the closing of the age. These conditions have marked all the centuries since the Lord in his resurrected body ascended into glory. These things are only the beginning of sorrows, and will be succeeded by far worse conditions before the Son of man comes to set up his kingdom.

Now, if wars and divisions and troubles are not specific signs of the end of the age and of the return of Christ Jesus in glory, then what are we to look for as being those prophetic events that herald the near-coming of our Lord? As the Spirit of God shall help us, let us search out some of those signs in Holy Scripture.

The Return of the Jew to the Holy Land in Unbelief

In answer to the question of the disciples, "When shall these things be? and what shall be the sign of thy coming and of the end of the world?" our Lord gave the parable of the budding fig tree (Matt. 24:32-34). The most important sign, then, has to do with the restoration of the Jews to the land of Palestine. The fig tree in Scripture represents the nation of Israel (Matt. 21:19; 1 Kings 4:25). Just as men know that summer is approaching by the appearance of leaves on the fig trees, so men can know that Christ's coming is near by the evidences of life in Israel. The Israelites have been scattered for centuries and have had no national existence, but today they are returning to their holy land.

No single event in our present generation has greater significance than the restoration of the nation of Israel to her earthly inheritance. The fig tree is bringing forth its green leaves. It is a remarkable thing that we should be living in that age when these things are beginning to come to pass before our very eyes. Jesus foretold all of this under the figure and parable of the miraculously withered but again-to-be-restored fig tree (Matt. 21:18-20). We have seen how the fig tree was dried up from the roots, but the root itself, which is the covenant God made by grace with Abraham, Israel, and Jacob, has never been altered or changed. Even though the fig tree, Israel, has been withered for these nineteen hundred years since these words were spoken, nevertheless, the covenant is sure.

So, the Jew is returning to the land according to the prophetic picture. Though thrilled with the new spirit of nationalism, he remains in his blindness (Rom. 11:25) and unbelief—a rejector of his Messiah and King. Peter in Acts 3:19-26 clearly states that the national repentance of Israel must precede their national blessings promised by the prophets. Their national sin, demanding a national repentance, was the sin of rejecting and crucifying their Messiah, the Christ. During this present church age, the nation is temporarily set aside while the church is being called out. But as soon as that body of Christ is complete, God will set his hand to fulfill all his promises to establish Israel forever.

From the time of Abraham, the state of Israel has been an important barometer of the movement of God upon the pages of human history. When God made a covenant with Abraham, he promised Palestine to the Jews as their inheritance (Gen. 12:1-3;15:5,18; Ps. 105:8-11). He promised blessing to the nation for obedience, but chastening for disobedience, and because of their disobedience, he took the Jews out of their land. The northern kingdom was captured by Assyria and the southern kingdom by Babylonia. After the Babylonian Captivity the Jews were permitted to come back to the land, although only a remnant returned.

In the time of Christ, the Jews were under Roman rule. They rejected their Messiah and crucified him. Their city and Temple were destroyed by the Romans in A.D. 70, and they were expelled again from their land. So, from the time of the Babylonian invasion (606 B.C.) to the present day, Palestine has been under the authority of the Gentiles. For the past nineteen hundred years almost all of Israel has been scattered to the four corners of the world among the nations, even as the Lord prophesied, "They shall fall by the edge of the sword, and shall be led away captive into all nations: and Jerusalem shall be trodden down of the Gentiles, until the times of the Gentiles be fulfilled" (Luke 21:24). The Jews have been hated, persecuted, and oppressed. Attempts to exterminate them have been tried over and over again, but in spite of all these efforts, they have never perished. In the plan of God the Jew has been preserved through both captivities and also through the dispersion of the New Testament.

This people, scattered among the Gentiles, has now been established in their homeland as an independent nation, recognized by the world. They have their own flag, their own government, their own army and navy, their own currency, and their own constitution. For many years men have thought that God was through with the nation Israel. They have said that the Jews will never return as a nation again. All of these prognostications have been proved wrong. God only can be right.

This is significant for us because during the tribulation period, Israel will be back in her land in unbelief. She will be oppressed by other nations and will be looking for any new leader who can settle her dispute. The nation, in her tragic plight, will be ready to receive the Antichrist and his covenant (Dan. 9:27) to protect them. But actually no one, not even the United Nations, will be able to settle their disputes. They will be settled by no one but the Lord Jesus Christ when he returns. Truly, the fig tree beginning to bud heralds the approach of our Lord—the fact that there is an independent nation of Israel in the land of Palestine. And this nation will be spiritually born in a day upon the return of the Lord (Rom. 11:25-29).

If the budding of the fig tree (Israel) is a sign of the imminent coming of Christ, the signs of their resurrection in the valley of dry bones is no less so. In Ezekiel 37, the prophet had a vision of a valley of dry bones. This prophecy is in the process of fullfillment before our very eyes today in the political restoration of Israel as a nation. The prophet was carried away in a vision to a valley filled with bones that were very dry (Ezek. 37:1-10). He was told to prophesy to these bones, and as he did, there was a noise among the bones, then a shaking, then a movement of the bones, then flesh and sinew covered the restored skeletons. But the bodies were still dead. There was no spirit in them. The prophet was then commanded to prophesy to the wind. As he did, life entered into the bodies; they moved and breathed and stood upon their feet.

The interpretation of this amazing vision is given in the verses that follow. Many people spiritualize the scene and make it apply to the church, or to the individual, or to our own nation, but list to God's interpretation of this vision:

"Then he said unto me, Son of man, these bones are the whole house of Israel: behold, they say, Our bones are dried, and our hope is lost: we are cut off for our parts.

Therefore prophesy and say unto them, Thus saith the Lord God; Behold, O my people, I will open your graves, and cause you to come up out of your graves, and bring you into the land of Israel" (Ezek. 37:11-12).

God is saying that the time is coming when those bones, the nation of Israel, shall be gathered out of the graves of the nations and will go back into their land. Notice that in the resurrection of these dry bones there are two stages.

The first stage is a noise among the bones, a shaking, a moving of bone to bone—flesh and sinews appear and skin covers the body. This stage is already beginning to happen. Israel, as a nation, is going back to the land of Palestine and the nation is organized, but the return has been, thus far, only political.

The second stage is found in spiritual revival, a revival which will not come until the Messiah appears upon the scene. It is not until the prophet is told to prophesy to the wind, and commands breath to enter the body, that life appears. This is the breathing of the Spirit of God into this politically but spiritually dead nation. "And I shall put my spirit in you, and ye shall live, and I shall place you in your own land: then shall ye know that I the Lord have spoken it, and performed it, saith the Lord" (Ezek. 37:14). The first stage, the recognition of Israel by the nations, is already fulfilled. We wait now for the next stage, the coming of the King to bring new birth to the people. This is in keeping with Ezekiel 36:24, when the prophet tells of Israel's return to the land, a prophecy which is immediately followed by another one in verse 26—namely, her conversion at the second coming.

"For I will take you from among the heathen, and gather you out of all countries, and will bring you into your own land.

"A new heart also will I give you, and a new spirit will I put within you: and I will take away the stony heart out of your flesh, and I will give you an heart of flesh" (Ezek. 36:24,26).

The apostle Paul confirms this national conversion in Romans 11:26.

Now in our generation, all of these things are beginning to happen. The Scriptures tell us that when these things happen, the coming of the Lord is very near. If there were no other sign of the last days, this one alone would be sufficient. But there are yet other mighty signs. Let us look at them.

The Sign of the Rise of Russia

The rise of Russian influence is another significant factor of the buds that would indicate that the coming of the Lord may be very near. After the First World War the land of Palestine was freed from Turkish rule. After the Second World War the land of Palestine was opened for the return of the Jews. The reshuffling of the nations is preparing the way for the fulfillment of God's Word concerning the end of the Gentile age.

God's revelation concerning the northern confederacy, Russia and her allies, is in Ezekiel 38 and 39. Gog is the name of a leader, and Magog is his land, so in these chapters we see God's wrath against a man and his land. In Genesis 10 we find the names of these people to be the descendants of Japheth who settled in the area that we know today as Russia (the region above the Caucasus mountains). "The King of the North" (Ezek. 38:19; 39:2) is Russia. When the Jews are settled in the land, they will become an object of attack by this formidable foe. The only reason the Soviet Union has not already moved in on Israel is fear of annihilation by atomic warfare. But when God's hour strikes, Russia will take the risk (Joel 2:20).

Russian Communism is the power that dominates a large portion of the world's population today, particularly in the Middle East. This has taken place within my lifetime. A few years ago this prophecy of Ezekiel seemed remote, but today we have seen many countries taken over by Russia, brought under the hammer and sickle. We are today living in the very day of the fulfillment of these prophecies. And Russia still marches on!

In Ezekiel 37 we see the prophecy of Israel's restoration. In Ezekiel 40 we see Israel's kingdom rest and blessing after the second coming of Christ. Between these two chapters we have Ezekiel 38 and 39, which is Russia's attack on Israel and Russia's defeat. God destroys her as he destroyed Sodom and Gomorrah. When does Russia invade Israel? When Israel is dwelling safely in the land (Ezek. 38:8), resting on the covenant the Antichrist has made with her, promising her security and protection. The attack will be after the restoration (Ezek. 37) and before Israel's final establishment in the land under the reign of Christ (Ezek. 40). Russia will be defeated in the tribulation period (Ezek. 38:18-22). Before this invasion takes place, Jesus is coming for the church (Rev. 3:10). In Luke 21:28 our Lord said, after he described the coming tribulation during which this invasion takes place, "And when these things [the things that herald the tribulation] begin to come to pass, then look up, and lift up your heads; for your redemption draweth nigh." Keep your eyes on the Middle East, for the fear of another world war will be centered in that area. Armageddon is located there. Our blessed hope (the rapture) will be next on the program for us, and then God himself will take a hand in settling the affairs of the nations.

The Sign of the Rise of China

Revelation 16:10-16 describes "the battle of that great day of God Almighty" called in Revelation 16:16 "Armageddon." In the prophecy, in verse 12 of Chapter 16, reference is made to "the kings of the east." The whole world, then, will be involved in that war, and that includes the Communist world of China and her satellites. With the Communist takeover of China, the real sleeping giant of Asia was awakened. In the twenty-odd years since the fall of China to the Communists, there has been a steady preparation for all-out war with the free world. They have made fearful progress in the production of weapons for war.

While Russia now apparently believes that the free world can be captured by the relatively limited violence of internal subversion (which masquerades under the guise of "peaceful coexistence"), the Chinese insist that the world can be conquered only by force of arms and by violence. But neither has disembarked from the total goal of world conquest for Communism. Without the absolute destruction of the capitalist system, the basic goal of Communism could not be attained; that is, the changing of man's nature by the complete change of his environment. Because of the Communist Chinese belief that the free world can only be overthrown by all-out war, they have for years devoted much of their military budget to developing nuclear weapons. They went from the testing of a crude atomic bomb to the successful test firing of an H-bomb in two-

and-one-half years. We believe, therefore, that China is
the beginning of the formation of the great conglomerate
called "the kings of the east." We believe that another
sphere of political power is forming its predicted role in
the final stages of history leading to the battle of Armageddon.

The Sign of a United, Federated Europe

Another significant event that points to the near return
of our Lord is the rise of a coalition of nations under a
common head, the Antichrist, to fulfill the prophecies of
Daniel 2 and 7 and Revelation 13. This will be a federation
of ten nations. The *number* is mentioned in three different
prophecies; (1) the ten toes of Nebuchadnezzar's image
in Daniel 2; (2) the ten horns of the Beast in Daniel 7;
(3) the Beast pictured with ten horns in Revelation 13. This
ten-kingdom federation will be a revival of the ancient
Roman Empire. We see from the image of Daniel 2 that
the land of Palestine throughout her course of history
would be dominated by Babylonia, Medo-Persia, Greece,
and Rome, and we see the final form of the Roman Empire
represented by the ten toes of the image and by the ten
horns of the Beast in Daniel 7. We see in all of this a
union of nations which is the outgrowth of the old Roman
Empire. Because of Russia's rise to power, those nations
will unite as a protection against "the king of the north."
It is this fear that drives the nations to the fullfillment
of the prophecies of God's Word.

What is happening in Europe today is not simply a
cooperation of nations for economic relief. The European
economic community is reaching toward full political
union. An article in the December, 1972, *European Community* magazine stated:

The statesmen who proposed and negotiated the . . . European economic community saw a politically united Europe as the ultimate goal of their endeavors. The nine heads of government of the nations, which will make up the enlarged community in 1973, have reinforced that aim in a communique following their summit meeting in Paris: "The member states of the community . . . affirm their intention to transform, before the end of the present decade, the whole complex of their relations into a European Union."

By reconstructing a mighty government out of the ruins of the ancient Roman Empire, the Antichrist will have accomplished what no one else has been able to do since A.D. 476, the year the Roman Empire officially died. Charlemagne tried to put it back together, but failed. Napoleon did his best, but met his Waterloo. Hitler envisioned the Mediterranean Sea as a "German lake" and the whole world as his empire. His efforts resulted in the downfall of his own nation. But what these would-be dictators could not do, world forces are achieving in bringing Europe together.

One of the motivating factors in forming this economic community is the concern over a common enemy. An article about "Mister Europe at Eight" quotes Jean Monnet, called the father of the Common Market, as saying: "As long as Europe remains divided, it is no match for the Soviet Union. Europe must unite."

Another reason for the Common Market is seen in the fact that Europeans sense the basic weakness of the United States in its will to resist Communism. They seem to realize that if Europe were really at stake, the United States would be dragging its feet in reacting against a Russian invasion.

Still another reason for the Common Market is the realization of the great potential of a united Europe. Former Secretary of State Dean Rusk said:

Powerful forces are moving in the European community toward a political integration. Survival and growth force the nations of Europe to forget their antagonism and unite. Through the pooling of the resources and efforts a mighty new entity is growing out of the chaos left by national rivalries and world wars.

It is no wonder, therefore, that men who have studied prophecy for years believe that the basic beginning of the unification of Europe has begun.

In these conflicts between mighty world powers, Russia, China, a united Europe, and the aligned nations of the world, east and west, north and south, we have the background for dictatorship, a striving for world conquest, *and finally Armageddon.*

To have a commanding, dominating government, there must be a leader, a superman (the Beast, the Antichrist, the man of sin) who will receive his power from the devil (Rev. 13:2). Christ's return will not occur until this man is revealed (2 Thess. 2:3-4) and this man will demand worship of himself. According to Daniel's prophecy (Dan. 9:27), the Israeli leader and the Antichrist will sign an agreement; then the seventieth week will begin the Jewish clock again. God will start dealing with the nation, Israel, again when "the fullness of the Gentiles" has come in (Rom. 11:25). Thus, the tribulation period starts with the agreement or covenant the Jews have made with death and hell (Isa. 28:15-18). "He shall confirm the covenant with many for one week: and in the midst of the week he shall cause the sacrifice and the oblation to cease" (Dan. 9:27). This Antichrist will proclaim himself as God.

"Let no man deceive you by any means: for that day shall not come, except there come a falling away first, and that man of sin be revealed, the son of perdition;

Who opposeth and exalteth himself above all that is called God, or that is worshipped; so that he as God sitteth

in the temple of God, shewing himself that he is God"
(1 Thess. 2:3-4).

As this spirit of man-worship grows, antagonism against
God will be more manifest until finally humanity, as expressed through this last mighty government, will be in
war against God himself. The affairs of our world will
be in such confusion that people will be ready for any
new Caesar, any new Hitler, any new deity that will promise peace and security to our world. Thus, we are marching
on to the near-return of our Lord. Our Savior said in Luke
21:25, "And there shall be signs in the sun, and in the
moon, and in the stars; and upon the earth distress of
nations, with perplexity; the sea and the waves roaring."
What better description could we have of the present
international situation? "The distress of the nations!" A
few years ago we thought the United Nations would be
a solution to the problems of war. It was a vain hope,
like the victory of the Allies in World War I, fought "to
end all wars." Facing even greater conflicts we have no
ultimate hope but in the return of the Prince of peace,
King Jesus.

The Sign of the Great Apostasy

In 2 Thessalonians 2:3 we are told that: "That day [the
day of the Lord] shall not come, except there come a falling
away first." The "falling away" is evidenced on every hand.
The Scriptures speak of the great apostasy, the falling
away from the true faith to a false gospel. "But there were
false prophets also among the people, even as there shall
be false teachers among you, who privily shall bring in
damnable heresies, even denying the Lord that bought
them, and bring upon themselves swift destruction" (2
Peter 2:1). Paul forewarned the Ephesians in Acts 20:29,
"For I know this, that after my departing shall grievous

wolves enter in among you, not sparing the flock." The
apostle John also tells us that in his day there were many
Antichrists denying the Father and the Son (I John
2:18-19).

The picture of the final church of Laodicea in Revelation
3:14-20 shows Christ knocking at the door for admission.
This is the church that is supposed to preach the Lord
Jesus, but where is Christ? Not on the inside but on the
outside. The church is lukewarm and claims to be rich
and increased with goods and in need of nothing. But
Christ says, "Thou art wretched, and miserable, poor and
naked and blind" (v. 17). This Laodicean church will be
so influenced by the mad rush for wealth and pleasure
that it will be almost engulfed by it. It will lose all spiritual
power and understanding, so it will be rejected. This is
one of the significant signs of the day in which we live.
This dreadful apostasy has swept in like a flood. Many
of the churches which in days past taught the true Word
of God have repudiated the authority of the Scriptures
and are teaching false doctrine.

For one thing, the churches have fallen prey to ecclesiastical liberalism. Ecclesiastical liberalism is that form of
doctrine which claims to be Christian but is a complete
perversion of Bible teachings. Satan has tried to pervert
the truth by giving a false interpretation to every doctrine.
He has succeeded. Many seminaries have become cemeteries where Christian faith is buried. Theological professors who proclaim their doubts concerning the inspiration
of the Bible have so undermined the faith of the masses
that the great truths of the Bible have no longer a firm
hold on their hearts. What is the matter with the church
today? It is not fulfilling the Great Commission of Christ.
It has become just another betterment agency in the world.

Paul says: "There be some that trouble you, and would
pervert the gospel of Christ. But though we, or an angel

from heaven, preach any other gospel unto you than that which we have preached unto you, let him be accursed" (Gal. 1:7-8).

Paul calls this shifted emphasis a perversion of the true gospel and he lays the blame on false teachers. They themselves have rejected the great doctrine of redemption. This "perverted gospel" is called "the social gospel," which is not the gospel of Christ. The gospel of Christ seeks to transform men by regeneration of the Spirit. The "social gospel" aims to improve society through a "human betterment" program. The gospel of Christ is a message of redemption through the blood of Jesus. The social gospel is the message of social reform. The gospel of Christ is by faith. The social gospel is by works. These apostate leaders are described by Jude in Jude 16-19. All of this unbelief will increase and grow darker until the Antichrist appears. Paul says the great apostasy is a sure sign of the soon return of our Lord.

We are told in the Word that professing Christianity, which almost from its beginning was corrupted by false doctrines, will continue to wax worse and worse, until finally, disowned by God, it is destroyed by the Beast (Rev. 17:16-17). The last view that Scripture gives of currupted Christianity is under the symbol of a drunken woman, decked in scarlet and pearls seated on a Beast with a cup in her hand full of all abominations. The Beast is the mighty empire of the future, the ten horns are his ten kingdoms, and the woman is corrupt and apostate Christianity in its final stage. Their fake Christianity, combined with astrology, witchcraft, and other evils, is preparing the world for the establishment of the "great whore."

The Sign of Modern Black Arts

Some of the earliest known literature is books on the

black arts and astrology. All of these things were practiced by the Babylonians, the Medo-Persians, the Greeks, and then the Romans. Israel was taken into Babylonian captivity because the people were given over to idolatry. Let us see what God says about these wizards, enchanters, and charmers: "There shall not be found among you any one that maketh his son or his daughter to pass through the fire, or that useth divination, or an observer of times, or an enchanter, or a witch, Or a charmer, or a consulter with familiar spirits, or a wizard, or a necromancer" (Deut. 18:10-11).

We are seeing the revival of Mystery Babylon today in astrology, spiritism, drugs, and the hallucination of the supernatural. "In the latter times some shall depart from the faith, giving heed to seducing spirits, and doctrines of devils" (1 Tim. 4:1). In speaking of the great false religion, John writes in Revelation 18:23, "by thy sorceries were all nations deceived." The word *sorcery* comes from the Greek word *pharmakeia* from which we get our English word, *pharmacy*. It is an occult worship associated with drugs. Just look at our world today and the spread of drug addiction and what it has done to our youth and young adults. It reduces a person's mentality to the point where he is easily demon-possessed. As we forsake the true God and turn to astrology (no modern newspaper would dare publish an edition without a column on this witchcraft) and the black arts we are laying the foundation for the final dissolution of a godly society. This is a part of the great apostasy.

The Last Sign and Warning

Let us look at Matthew 24:37-39 for the last sign.

"But as the days of Noe were, so shall also the coming

of the Son of man be.

For as in the days that were before the flood they were eating and drinking, marrying and giving in marriage, until the day that Noe entered into the ark,

And knew not until the flood came, and took them all away; so shall also the coming of the Son of man be."

For over 100 years Noah was warning of judgment to come. He warned that a flood would destroy all unbelievers. He preached the longest sermon in the history of preaching and did not have one convert outside of his own family. Why would not people receive the message of salvation? Because they were so occupied with the things of life—eating, drinking, marrying, selling, planting, building, and ever learning the things of this world, not the things of God.

Daniel wrote of our age when he said, "Knowledge shall be increased" (Dan. 12:4). There is great advancement in our twentieth century in every department of learning, and especially in the sciences. We have public schools for our youth, colleges and universities for higher education, and denominational schools for religious education. We have a wonderful wealth of "new knowledge" in the fields of medicine, radio, television, chemistry, electronics, mechanics, and biology. All of these things remind us of the end of the age.

Daniel also wrote that "many shall run to and fro" (Dan. 12:4). Our modern system of rapid transit, railway, automobiles, buses, and airplanes has enhanced the desire to travel. It seems to be the goal of a large part of the population to go and go—just to be going.

What is sinful about doing these things? The sinful thing is that the antediluvians were so occupied with things like these that they missed the truth of God. Yes, they missed the warning signs of judgment and had no place in the ark. People, likewise, are so busy today with the so-called "good things of life" that they have no time to worship God. They are so busy building homes for themselves that they neglect securing a home in heaven. So, just as suddenness characterized the visitation of judgment in Noah's day, so will suddenness mark the last hour of this present age (Luke 17:26-27).

We are also told that Jesus' coming will be similar to the destruction of Sodom. Lot was told by two angels that God was going to bring judgment on Sodom. He was mercifully saved only when the angels took him and his family out of the city to safety. Then God poured down fire and brimstone on the city, while the people were engaged in their sinful, worldly pursuits (Luke 17:28-30). Our Lord warned:

"I tell you, in that night there shall be two men in one bed; the one shall be taken, and the other shall be left.

Two women shall be grinding together; the one shall be taken, and the other left.

Two men shall be in the field; the one shall be taken, and the other left" (Luke 17:34-36).

The whole earth is moving toward the vast consummation of the age. There is not another thing to be fulfilled in order for us to say, "Come, Lord Jesus!" Any minute, any day, any hour, he may come for his own to save us from the awesome judgments of "The Great Tribulation."

11
The Coming King

When Jesus of Nazareth was brought to trial, the Roman governor of Judea was loathe to get involved in the case. Pilate at first said, "Take ye him, and judge him according to your law."

But the accusors of the Messiah sought the death penalty and appealed to Pilate that he, having the power to exact capital punishment, hear the case. Thus, this minor official of a Roman province sought to interrogate the mind of Christ.

"Then Pilate entered into the judgment hall again, and called Jesus, and said unto him, Art thou the King of the Jews? Jesus answered him, Sayest thou this thing of thyself, or did others tell it thee of me? Pilate answered, Am I a Jew? Thine own nation and the chief priests have delivered thee unto me: what hast thou done? Jesus answered, My kingdom is not of this world: if my kingdom were of this world, then would my servants fight, that I should not be delivered, but now is my kingdom not from hence. Pilate therefore said unto him, Art thou a king then? Jesus answered. Thou sayest that I am a king. To this end was I born, and for this cause came I into the world" (John 18:33-37).

As we have seen, Jesus most emphatically identified himself as a king. And surely, true to the Scriptures, he

is the covenant-promised King of Israel. God's uncondi-
tional guarantee gave to Abraham, Isaac, Jacob, and their
seed the land of Israel for an everlasting possession. The
same Lord God promised to David that he would have
a descendant who would reign upon his throne forever.

The prophet Isaiah sang of that glorious son of King
David in these terms: "For unto us a child is born, unto
us a son is given: and the government shall be upon his
shoulder: and his name shall be called Wonderful, Counsellor, The mighty God, The everlasting Father, The Prince
of Peace. Of the increase of his government and peace,
there shall be no end, upon the throne of David, and upon
his kingdom, to order it, and to establish it with judgment
and his justice henceforth even for ever. The zeal of the
Lord of hosts will perform this" (Isa. 9:6-7).

Jesus, David's descendant, was indeed born a king, the
mighty King prophesied throughout the old covenant. And
Pontius Pilate, whatever his intentions, indeed sentenced
a king to death.

The King Is Born

Some 750 years after Isaiah's prophecy the angel Gabriel
was sent to the little town of Nazareth, in Galilee, to the
Jewish virgin, Mary. And there he announced to her the
stupendous news that she would be the mother of that
foretold and foreordained child: "And the angel answered
and said unto her, The Holy Ghost shall come upon thee,
and the power of the Highest shall overshadow thee: therefore also that holy thing which shall be born of thee shall
be called the Son of God" (Luke 1:35). "He shall be great,
and shall be called the Son of the Highest: and the Lord
God shall give unto him the throne of his father David.
And he shall reign over the house of Jacob for ever; and
of his kingdom there shall be no end" (vv. 32-33).

Then upon a night of nights, when the heavens were
filled with the harmony of the glory of God, when the
very air was filled with the rhythm and resonance of the
singing of God's created hosts in glory, when each star
seemed to be let down like a golden lamp close to the
earth, the child was born. An angel came from heaven
and announced to the startled shepherds that they would
find the child in Bethlehem. They were to go see him
for themselves. Then the heavens rolled back like a scroll
and the angelic choir that had been waiting since the dawn
of creation flung upward to the heavenly throne their
adoration, "Glory to God in the highest." Then they flung
downward to the waiting earth their benediction, "On
earth, peace, good will toward men."

The King was born.

Behold, the King

In the fifteenth year of Tiberius Caesar, Luke tells us,
Jesus, about thirty years of age at that time, was baptized
in the Jordan River by John the Baptist. After that he
went forth to announce to the world and to Israel the
coming kingdom and to present himself as the coming
king. He carried with him the credentials of his claim.
Through his mother Mary he was descended from David
through the line of Solomon. Through Joseph, the husband
of Mary, he was descended from David through the line
of Nathan. By legal right, by birth, by covenant promise,
he was a king.

There came wise men from the east to Jerusalem saying,
"Where is he that is born King of the Jews?"

He carried with him the credentials of a sinless life.
He carried with him the credentials of matchless and incomparable words. He carried with him the credentials
of miraculous and marvelous deeds.

At the exact moment the angel had foretold to Daniel the prophet, in the exact manner as foretold by Zechariah, the King of glory and Prince of peace came riding into the Holy City of Jerusalem, there to present himself as the promised and covenant King. As he rode into the city, the multitudes on every side lifted their voices in praise to the coming King. "Hosannah," they cried, in the highest. Hosannah to the Son of David. "Blessed be the King that cometh in the name of the Lord."

When the scribes and Pharisees heard these words of adulation, they urged the disciples to quiet the throng, but the Lord replied, "If these should hold their peace, the stones would immediately cry out." The covenant moment in world history had arrived. The King had come.

Jesus, the Son of God, presented himself as the promised, covenant, coming King of Israel.

The King Is Crucified

When he was betrayed and arrested, he was arraigned before the Sanhedrin, the highest court of the Jewish nation. The presiding officer, the chief justice of the court, placed Jesus on the witness stand and stated, "I adjure thee by the living God, that thou tell us whether thou be the Christ, the Son of God." And the Lord replied, "Thou hast said. . . . Hereafter shall ye see the Son of man sitting on the right hand of power and coming in the clouds of heaven." And when the Lord so answered under oath, the High Priest rent his garments and said to his fellow members of the Sanhedrin, "Ye have heard his blasphemy. What think ye?" The Sanhedrin replied, "He is guilty of death" (Matt. 26:63-66).

The Jews were no longer empowered to perform the execution so they took the Lord and arraigned him before Pontius Pilate. There they accused him of treason and sedition saying that he called himself a king. And Pilate asked him, "Art thou the King of the Jews?" The Lord answered, "Thou sayest" (Matt. 26:11).

Then Pilate turned to the Jewish nation and said, "Behold your King." Pilate questioned, "Shall I crucify your king?" And the mob replied, "Away with him. Crucify him. We have no king but Caesar. Away with him. Let him be crucified" (see John 19:14-15).

Thus he was crucified a king. He died a king. The superscription of his accusation was written for the whole world to read in Greek and in Latin and in Hebrew. The Roman governor wrote, "This is Jesus the King of the Jews" (Matt. 27:37).

"He came unto his own, and his own received him not" (John 1:11).

The King Is Exiled

Jesus taught a clear parable in the nineteenth chapter of Luke concerning a nobleman who went away into a far country, there to receive a kingdom for himself. And he said to his subjects, "Occupy till I come" (v. 13).

This is the position we find ourselves in as subjects, occupying a kingdom, awaiting the great covenant and consummating moment when God shall intervene in human history and the King shall return.

We are waiting in an interlude. The kingdom has been postponed to some future day. God has chosen to create a great intermission. The kingdom shall come and the purposes of God will be consummated, but in the meanwhile we occupy in the place of an exiled King. It was God's secret untold by the Old Testament prophets and kept in the heart of God until the day that he revealed it to his holy apostles. There is to be an intermission, an interlude between the death of the Lord and the consummation, the coming kingdom.

How Satan must have exalted the day the Son of God
was crucified on the cross. Israel has killed her own Son!
The chosen people wallow blindly in unbelief and rejection! Every promise and prophecy of God shall fall to
the ground! There is no kingdom, and there shall be no
king. Death shall reign forever. Satan shall be crowned
forever, and sin shall rule forever. The world shall be
plunged without amelioration, without alleviation, without
hope, into darkness and death forever. How Satan must
have rejoiced in the day of the cross when the Son of
God died like a felon hanged on a tree!

But in the grand design and purpose of God, the death
of Christ was seen from eternity past. It served as the means
by which atonement would be made for the sin of the
people. Out of that atoning death God intended from
eternity past to bring forth a new creation.

The apostle Paul reveals in Ephesians 3 that God's
eternal purpose, though kept secret from the Old Testament prophets, was that this day in which we live is
to be the day of grace. It is the day of the Holy Spirit.
It is the day of the church when God is calling out a new
body of believers and creating a new fellowship. In this
new creation there is to be Jew and Gentile, bond and
free, male and female, old and young, learned and un-
learned. They come out of all the nations and tribes and
kingdoms of the world. They are now engrafted into the
holy olive tree. By invitation, anyone in this day of grace
can become a member of the household of faith, a member
of the chosen family of God. This is the day of the preaching of the gospel of the grace of the Son of God. To the
ends of the earth, any man who hears the voice of the
Lord, who feels the wooing and invitation of the Holy
Spirit, who names the name of Jesus Christ, can become

a member of the chosen family of God.

The King of the Future

As we have said, we do not have our kingdom now, and we do not have our King. In our day God is surely creating a new body, the church of Jesus Christ, the Bride of our Lord. But the kingdom and the King are yet in the future.

Jesus is not the King of the church. There is no such nomenclature in the Bible. He is the head of the church, and we are members of his body. But he is never called King of the church.

What of the kingdom, and what of the King? That was what the apostles asked the Lord Jesus when he was ascending up into heaven, "Wilt thou at this time restore again the kingdom to Israel?" (Acts 1:6). And the thief who was crucified with the Lord Jesus turned to him and said, "Lord, remember me when thou comest into thy kingdom" (Luke 23:42).

Many of those who encountered the Lord asked about the kingdom and looked forward to the kingdom. Surely we still do that. Surely we still wait in hope for that coming kingdom. We wait to look upon the final fulfillment of all the prophecies and all the covenants and all of the promises of God. We wait to look upon the triumphant, glorious face of the King of the Jews, the King of the nations, the King of the universe, the King of kings. Like those in the scriptures who eagerly asked about the kingdom of heaven, we await it. And sometime in an hour known only to God, the heavens will be rolled back like a scroll, and the King of glory shall come through. According to the Scriptures, Christ our living, reigning Lord shall come down and institute his kingdom.

The King is coming.

Caught Up!—The Rapture of the Church

He is coming first as a thief in the night. Then he is coming, according to the Scriptures, as the livid lightning splits the bosom of the sky. In that glorious consummating hour we shall see him personally and visibly descending from the sky.

The remarkable simile of a thief in the night expresses Jesus coming to steal away his pearl of price, to take out of the world his jewels, the treasures hid in the earth. He is coming clandestinely, furtively, secretly, with sandled feet. He is coming to take away, to rapture his people without announcement, without placard, without advertisement. We shall be "caught up!" No one knows the moment or the hour he will come. It can be anytime, any day, any second. It can be at high noon or at midnight. It can be at dawn or in twilight. All of us shall share in the glory of that triumph and that moment, as we have said. God shall speak to those who have fallen asleep in the Lord and who have been buried in the heart of the earth, and they shall rise to live again in his sight. We who are alive and remain unto his coming shall be changed in a moment, in the twinkling of an eye, at the last trump. For the trumpet shall sound and the dead in Christ shall be raised incorruptible. We shall all be changed.

There shall not be a bone left in the region of death, not a relic for Satan to gloat over. We shall all be changed, caught up to meet our Lord in the air. Two shall be sleeping in a bed; one shall be taken, the other left. Two shall be grinding at a mill, one shall be taken and the other left. Two shall be working in a field, one shall be taken, the other left. Without notice, without harbinger, suddenly the Lord shall come for his people.

Nor can the tribulation and judgment fall upon the earth until first his people be delivered out of it. It was only after Noah was *in* the ark safely that the judgment fell. It was only after Lot was snatched out of Sodom did the fire and brimstone fall. Nor can there be judgment upon the earth as long as his people live in it.

But there shall come a day as it was in the days of Noah, as it was in the days of Lot, when God shall take out of the world his people. He shall rapture his church, and then shall the tribulation come, and then shall the judgment fall. Then at the end of that period of judgment and tribulation shall the heavens be rolled back like a scroll, and then the Lord who has already come *for* his people shall descend *with* the redeemed of all glory.

The King and His Kingdom

As Jude says, "Behold the Lord cometh with ten thousands of his saints" (v. 14). And as the text of Revelation 1:7 says, "Behold, he cometh with clouds; and every eye shall see him, and they also who pierced him: and all kindreds of the earth shall wail because of him. Even so, Amen."

The Lord shall come openly and visibly and personally, and every eye shall see him, for the Lord God is coming in triumph to be king over all God's creation. The earth, the planets, the other galaxies, the universe, all of the handiwork of God shall bow in obeisance and adoration before the Lord God Christ, the coming King.

He is coming in the glory of the Father, as God the Son, and the Son of God.

He is coming in the glory of the angels as the Captain of the hosts of heaven.

He is coming in the glory of the church as the Bridegroom with the bride. He is coming in his own glory as the Son of God, the son of Abraham, the son of David, the Son of man, the virgin-born man, the crucified man, the risen man, the eternally manifest God-man, Christ Jesus.

He is coming to be the King of Israel and the King of the Jews and the King of the nations and the King of kings and the Lord of all the lords.

He is coming to be Lord God Almighty.

And he is coming to be the restorer and the re-creator of this earth.

When Christ shall come and remake this creation, then will be brought to pass those marvelous prophecies: "They shall beat their swords into plowshares, and their spears into prunning hooks: nation shall not lift up a sword against nation, neither shall they learn war any more. But they shall sit every man under his vine and under his fig tree; and none shall make them afraid" (Micah 4:3-4). "The wolf also shall dwell with the lamb, and the leopard shall lie down with the kid. . . . And the [carnivorous and ravenous] lion shall eat straw like an ox. They shall not hurt nor destroy in all my holy mountain: for the earth shall be filled with the knowledge of the Lord, as the waters cover the sea" (Isa. 11:6-7,9). God promises all of this and more when the King comes.

> Lo. He comes with clouds descending.
>   once for favored sinners slain.
> Thousands thousands saints attending,
>   swell the triumph of His train.
> Alleluhia, alleluhia,
>   God appears on earth to reign.
> Yea amen. Let all adore Thee
>   high on Thy eternal throne.
> Saviour, take the power and glory,
>   claim the kingdom for thine own.
> Oh come quickly, oh come quickly
>   everlasting God come down.
>
> —CHARLES WESLEY

12
The Rapture of
the Church

We have previously discussed Paul's marvelous message about the rapture of the church in connection with how it affected the dead in Christ. We saw that they would rise first, and that we need not sorrow as others who have no hope. At this point I would like to take up the translation of God's believing children, those who are caught up to meet the Lord in the air—all of the church, all of the believers.

This meaningful passage deserves repetition here:

"But I would not have you to be ignorant, brethren, concerning them which are asleep, that ye sorrow not, even as others which have no hope. For if we believe that Jesus died and rose again, even so them also which sleep in Jesus will God bring with him. For this we say unto you by the word of the Lord, that we which are alive and remain unto the coming of the Lord shall not prevent them which are asleep. For the Lord himself shall descend from heaven with a shout, with the voice of the archangel, and with the trump of God: and the dead in Christ shall rise first: Then we which are alive and remain shall be caught up together with them in the clouds, to meet the Lord in the air: and so shall we ever be with the Lord. Wherefore comfort one another with these words" (1 Thess. 4:13-18).

We will concern ourselves now with the translation of God-believing children, the rapture of his church, the immortalization, the transfiguration of living believers, and the resurrection of our beloved dead who sleep in Jesus. This passage is one of the most meaningful eschatological passages because it delineates and discusses in detail a further revelation of the most precious of all of the promises of our Lord. This revelation had been mentioned only once before, and that was from the lips of our blessed Savior. Thus, we will go back now to the life of our Lord and see exactly what it was that he said, and then we will better understand how Paul avows that this further revelation came from the same Lord Jesus himself.

The Messianic Kingdom

The Old Testament prophets spoke of the coming of our Lord endlessly. Almost the whole substance of their prophesying concerned the glory of the messianic kingdom and the exultation and wonder of the messianic King. From the start of the Old Testament Scriptures to the last syllable, the books are filled with those glorious prophetic utterances of the coming Lord and Savior and Redeemer and triumphant King.

But as we have said above, the only thing the Old Testament prophets never saw was this: They never saw an interval between two appearances of the Messiah. They just saw one. There is no exception to that. There was no Old Testament seer or preacher or prophet who saw other than that great, wonderful vision of the coming King. Sometimes they describe him as Isaiah did—a man lowly and acquainted with grief, a Lamb of God, a Suffering Servant by whose stripes we are healed. Yet the same prophet would describe the glory and the majesty of that incomparable servant of God, whom he names Wonderful,

Counsellor, the Mighty God, the Everlasting Father, the Prince of peace. They put it all together. To them it was one great prophetic promise and vision.

The disciples took the same view. They never saw an interval between the first and second messianic comings. The suffering Lamb of God came to die for the sins of the world. Then this long age called the age of the church, the age of the Spirit, dispensation of the Holy Ghost followed. But they never saw that. When the disciples heard the Baptist announce the Messiah was in their very midst, they were filled with all of those glorious expectations of the coming King and the establishment of the house of God among the nations and the exultation of Judea. One of them wanted to sit on his right hand; one of them wanted to sit on his left hand. He was to lead Israel out from under the bondage and the yoke of the Roman government and to establish forever a kingdom of Israel. And they certainly were ready for that!

When the disciples were filled with those glorious expectations, they were doing nothing but reflecting the Old Testament Scriptures that they loved and had read all of their lives. Can you imagine then the crestfallen despair that came upon the Lord's disciples when he began to tell them that he was to be slain, to be killed? It was inconceivable to their minds and their understanding. When actually and finally the Lord of glory died on the cross like a felon, like a criminal, like a malefactor—when finally Jesus was slain, and they looked at him in death—to them it was the end of the messianic hope. For them there expired in the death of Jesus every dream and every prophetic vision that they had read in the Bible and that they had loved and entertained in their hearts. For you see they did not realize—they had not come to know—that there was first a coming of our Lord in suffering and in humility when he took upon himself the diseases and sins and illnesses and infirmities of the people.

They could not from their point of view appreciate that one of these days, some glorious triumphant day, there will be another coming of the Lord in grace and in triumph and in mighty power, visible and open. He will establish a kingdom that shall abide forever and forever.

The Kingdom: A Mystery

In the third chapter of Ephesians, Paul describes that glorious interval that the prophets and the disciples never saw. He says that hidden in the counsels of God from the beginning of the world was this "mystery," as he terms it.

A *mystery* in the Bible is a secret known to God but which has been shared with those who are initiated. That is the meaning of the word *musterion* in the Greek language. The Greek mystery religions had secrets, like in a Masonic Lodge, and nobody knew them except they that were initiated. So Paul calls this great parenthesis (the age in which we now live) a *musterion*. It was something hidden in the counsels of God, that the prophets never saw, but it was revealed to the holy apostles. This *musterion* included the understanding of how Christ should die in the first appearing, how that the gospel of the Son of God should be preached to all of the world in this day and in this age, and that this age of grace should conclude with the glorious and marvelous personal triumph of Jesus over his enemies, shared by all of those who place their trust in him.

Now the Lord made that announcement to his apostles, who were filled with all of these visions of grandeur of the coming King and of the kingdom that would last forever (with they themselves on his right hand and left hand). So, when he made the announcement to them that he was to die, they were plunged into uncontrollable, indescribable grief and despair. And it was then that Jesus made the first revelation of this "mystery" that was to come to pass. We referred to it above as being the most precious of all the promises of our Lord.

"Let not your heart be troubled." No wonder they were troubled! Every hope and vision of their life was to be snuffed out in the crucifixion and death of their Lord and King: "Let not your heart be troubled. . . . In my Father's house are many mansions. . . . I go to prepare a place for you. And if I go and prepare a place for you, I will come again, and receive you unto myself; that where I am, there ye may be also" (John 14:1-3).

"I will come again." That is hardly the statement of a dying man. That simply does not describe death. This passage has been rendered a thousand false ways by those who cannot believe, or refuse to believe, that the Lord is simply coming again. But in death our disembodied spirits go to be with Jesus. He is coming for us. That is certainly not the destruction of Jerusalem, as some have asserted. ("Let not your hearts be troubled? I will come again in the destruction of Jerusalem?") That cannot be right. He is not referring to the destruction of the Roman Empire, nor scientific advancement and the spreading of scientific knowledge in the earth, nor a thousand other things that people say that it is. When he says, "I will come again," that is our Lord himself living and triumphant; our blessed Savior is coming for his own. And he told the disciples that in the shadow of the cross and in the midst of their grieving despair.

Now that is what Paul is further illustrating for us. "I will come again," and how shall it be? "This we say unto you by the word of the Lord," that we who are alive and remain in this world until that great and glorious and triumphant day comes shall all be caught up with God's sainted and resurrected dead. We shall be transformed, immortalized, transfigured, translated like Enoch was. Walking with the Lord and then suddenly there in the presence of God forever. We who are alive and remain shall be caught up with God's sainted dead to meet the Lord in the air when he comes for us.

A Miraculous Coming

"For the Lord himself shall descend from heaven," the Scripture says, and then Paul uses three unique descriptions. First, the Lord shall descend from heaven *en keleusma:* it is the Greek verb for command or signal, the word for the shout or the order of command. It was used in Greek to refer to a general giving a command to his army. It was also used to refer to an admiral addressing his oarsmen. It was used in Greek to refer to a charioteer as he drives his horses with shouts of command. The Lord shall descend from heaven with a shout. The Lord God shall speak and the dead shall arise incorruptible!

Think of the sovereignty and the power of the commanding, electing almighty sovereign God. Like someone once said, when the Lord Jesus stood at the tomb of Lazarus and said "Lazarus come forth," had he not specifically used the name Lazarus, the dead from the graveyards of the entire world would have arisen to come forth and meet the living Lord! God shall speak with a shout of command, and these graves shall be emptied! At the same time the living who trust in Jesus shall be raptured and translated, transformed in a moment, in the twinkling of an eye. The Lord himself shall descend from heaven with a shout, a shout of command—Arise—Arise—ARISE! Then the dead shall hear the voice of God and live again.

His coming is with a shout, with the voice (singular) of the archangel, *en phonei archangelos.* There is only one archangel in the Bible, and his name is Michael. To me that is one of the most unique revelations in all Scripture— that the Lord's coming is accompanied by the voice of Michael the Archangel. I have thought about that many times, and I think the reason is this: Michael's voice is the voice of victory and of triumph. It is Michael, after all, who wars against Satan, and Satan and his angels war against Michael. Ever since the Garden of Eden, Michael has been the defender of his people and the protector of Israel. And in this great and final day the shout of the Archangel Michael is a shout of glory and of triumph.

When Michael raises his voice, and Satan and death are vanquished with the voice of the archangel, there will also be the *salpingi theou,* the trumpet of God. Paul described that trumpet in 1 Corinthians 15:50 also. He began that passage, "This I say, brethren, flesh and blood cannot inherit the kingdom of God." As long as things are as they are now, we will never have the kingdom of God. As long as we are in this body of sin, we do not have a new body, nor shall we ever walk those golden streets in our impurity and iniquity. So, "Flesh and blood cannot inherit the kingdom of God; neither doth corruption inherit incorruption. Behold, I shew you a mystery [a *musterion*]" (v. 51). There the term is used again. Something was hidden in the heart of God that no man should ever know except by revelation. "I shew you a mystery [*musterion*]; We shall not all sleep. [Some of us are going to be alive when he comes. We shall not all sleep,] but we shall all be changed, in a moment, in the twinkling of an eye, at the last trump: for the trumpet shall sound, and the dead shall be raised incorruptible, and then we shall all be changed" (vv. 51-52). This gives a similar picture to 1 Thessalonians 4: We again see the trump of God and the dead in Christ rising first.

It is interesting to trace Paul's analogies. From where does he draw these exciting pictures: in a moment, in the twinkling of an eye, at the last trump? What is he referring to?

In the Roman army those marching legionaires were conquering and almost invincible. And in their military training there were three blastings of the trumpet. First, when the trumpet sounded in the middle of the night or the middle of the day at any hour, every Roman legionaire sprung to his feet and struck his tent. Then at the sounding of the second trumpet, every legionaire stood in line, ready to march. And at the sounding of the last trump, away and away and away did they march. That is what Paul means: the last trump. Time to march! Time to ride! Time to move!

O Jerusalem, O Israel, O church, and all the people of God, the glory of thy light is come, and the favor and blessing of the Lord God is upon thee. Arise, shine, put on thy beautiful garments. Oh, my soul, what a day, what a day!

One could preach quite a sermon on the blowing of the trumpet alone. If we were to look through the Bible for every blowing of the trumpet, we would see triumph and majesty in the purposes of God. The sermon would start with the blowing of the trumpet at Jericho, when on the seventh day and on the seventh time around the frontier-walled city they blew the trumpet and the walls of Jericho fell down. They fell at the glory of the trumpets of God.

The Hebrew people blew the trumpets at the beginning of a new year to celebrate a new day and a new hope. They blew the trumpets at the great Jubilee. They blew the trumpets when they went into battle, marching for God.

By Invitation Only

Who exactly is raised and who is translated on that great day? Certainly we understand that not all the dead will be raised. This is a selective, elective resurrection. Only those who hear the trumpet of God and the voice of the archangel and the shout of command from God, whose hearts have been turned to the Lord, will be raised. The rest do not hear. They are not raised. They lie in a Christless grave.

Each man must ask himself, what about me? Will I hear? Can I hear? Will the voice of God speak to my heart? Does the Spirit have a way into my soul?

If we can hear the voice of the Spirit of God, and open our hearts to the call and command of God at this time, then we will hear him again in that great day when he comes for his saints. But those who cannot hear now will not hear then. God must do something special in every life for this resurrection to be provided. If a human being dies and is buried and has never given his heart to the commands of God, when the day comes that the dead shall rise that one will be left. God's sainted dead will rise out of the dust of the ground, but the others shall stay buried in the earth until the judgment of the wicked dead described at the great white throne in Revelation 20. O God, blessed are they who have a part in the first resurrection, for upon them the second death shall have no power.

Do you hear the voice of the Lord? Do you hear the shout and command of God? Then respond with your life and someday you will respond from the grave if you fall before he comes.

Where will we go when we are raised? When he comes,

he is coming like a thief in the night, first to steal away
his jewels. In this earth is a treasure. He paid with his
life for it. We are a pearl of price. And he is coming without
announcement, like a thief in the night.

Paul says that we will meet him in the air. Then where
will we go? Well, we shall go to the place Jesus has prepared for us. We shall go to glory, to heaven, and we
shall sit down and share with our Lord the great marriage
supper of the Lamb. We shall be presented (and the Bible
uses the expression of a bride adorned in fine linen) clean
and white, without spot and without blemish. We shall
be presented to Jesus as a bride, living by his side, loved
in his sight.

When I think of that, I can just say glory, glory, glory!
Some will be blind, and when they are presented to Christ
they will see. Some will be deaf, and when they are presented they will hear. I know some crippled and lame,
but when they are presented to Jesus they will walk. And
I know of some poor, but when they are presented they
will be rich. I know some sinners, mostly myself, and when
we are presented, we shall be washed clean and white
in the blood of the Lamb.

Oh, glory, we are not waiting for the worms, and we
are not tarrying for death. We are not looking forward
just to the grave, the night, and the dark. We are lifting
up our eyes and turning our faces to the glorious sunrising
when the Lord shall be King of the earth and when we
shall reign by his side. O Jesus, blessed Savior!

And our deliverance, of course, our translation to heaven
is only the beginning. "Eye hath not seen, nor ear heard,
neither have entered into the heart of man, the things God
hath prepared for them that love him."

Let us open our hearts to God's voice of invitation. Let
us look up and trust.

13
When We All
Get to Heaven

What a wonderful future we all have in Jesus! What a literally "heavenly" regathering we have to look forward to!

In John, chapter ten, our Great Shepherd spoke in gracious terms of someday regathering his sheep to himself in heaven. He assured us, "I know my sheep," and he further said: "And other sheep I have, which are not of this fold: them also I must bring, and they shall hear my voice; and there shall be one fold, and one shepherd" (v. 16).

And the Lord further indicates that God's purposes of grace will be consummated when *all* the sheep are brought together; "And there shall be one fold, and one shepherd," Jesus stressed.

Think of it! All of us, from everywhere in the world—from the east and the west, from north and south; those who have fallen asleep in death believing in our Savior together with those who remain until he comes. Those of every nation will be included—all believers—both Jew and Gentile shall be gathered together in one fold with our one Savior.

There are so many facets of heaven about which a minister could preach. Heaven would make a joyous lifetime of sermons! But the facet especially meaningful to

me is this regathering of God's redeemed. "Other sheep
I have who are not of this fold," he said, speaking to an
entirely Jewish audience. "Other sheep."

Surely, they never had heard of America at that time
but God saw us here and called us by name even before
we were born. "Them also I must bring, and they shall
hear my voice; and there shall be one fold and one shepherd."

So, first of all heaven is a great *fellowship*. That is the
first thing I want to say about heaven—it is the "Fellowship
of fellowships!" Secondly, I am going to deal with the
fact that heaven must be chosen. We all have to make
our reservations individually—to plan ahead to go there,
as it were. And finally, I would like to describe heaven
as a situation purchased for us—bought with blood.

Heaven Is a Fellowship

Heaven is a *koinonia*, to use the Greek term, a gathering
together, a sharing together. Sometimes the word *koinonia*
is translated "fellowship," or "communion." Invariably it
means a gathering together—a sharing together—just what
it will be when all of God's people are finally shepherded
there to heaven.

God made us in such a way that we like to gather
together. The lonely Indians, scattered sparsely throughout
the plains and prairies of this vast land, held their pow-
wows, just to gather together. The Eskimo meets at some
central places from time to time for games, and for good
fellowship. Human beings, however remotely situated, invariably seek out each other's companionship.

Once I was driving through the desert stretches of Arizona, somewhere out in those thousands of acres of nothingness, and I came across the cabin of a cowboy. I just
had to stop and look it over; I hadn't seen any*thing* or

any*body* for quite awhile out there, after all. Well, the place was just a shack, so far away from everything and so modest, but there were pretty white starched curtains in the windows. And I thought to myself, "Inside that little house lives a cowboy's wife, and she has put those curtains there in the window for beauty's sake—but also she must have been hoping that somebody would drive down this lonely road and look at them."

That is not just a characteristic of women, but a general characteristic of people. The woman who hung those refreshing curtains in that desolate place was actually reaching out to people—passers-by, strangers. She was communicating in a simple kind of fellowship—"Aren't my curtains pretty?" "Don't they make you feel good as you glance from the roadway?" That woman had a natural desire to be with people, and that was the way she chose to do just that.

We don't have to go out into the country to find that hunger for fellowship. We're quite the same way in the city, as a matter of fact.

I was talking with an insurance man recently about his business. I asked him, "Who finally owns all those assets of a big insurance company like Metropolitan Life or New York Equitable?" He answered, "Theoretically, the last living, surviving policy holder. He owns it all!"

And I couldn't help but think to myself, "Oh, if I could just outlive everybody else! Think what I'd have if I were that last living policy holder!

"I'd have billions and billions of dollars. I'd have buildings, railroads, whole cities of my own!"

But then I stopped to consider. Who would live in my buildings and who would ride my railroads? I would own fleets of empty airplanes and armadas of empty ships. I would own empty hotels, with not a soul in the rooms, and empty houses, with no toys scattered in the yards and no people coming and going. There would only be me—and all that I owned.

My little fantasy had gone very sour very quickly. I ended up just thinking about how dreadful it would be if I were really completely alone. I am just like those Indians, those Eskimoes, and that dear lady of the Arizona plains. I am happy because *you* are here, and because we are together!

And that is true religion. There is a social side, a fellowship side to religion that has never varied through time. From the beginning it has been God's purpose that we gather together in his name. You can serve God all by yourself, I know. But God purposes for us to rejoice together. That is God's way of doing it.

Of course we are all going to be together by and by. In the Old Testament, how many times does the prophet teach that God will raise his people out of the dust of the ground, out of those dry-bone valleys? He will breathe into them the breath of life, and they shall be a standing army before the Lord, a living fellowship.

The concept remains the same in the New Testament also. For example, in those glorious visions of John in Revelation, he saw the new heaven and the new earth. "And there was no more sea" (21:1). Why did the Holy Spirit put that descriptive detail in Revelation? You must remember John had great affection for the people of the Lord. He was exiled on a lonely, rocky isle called Patmos. Between him and his beloved people in Ephesus were the waters of that sea. When he sees heaven and in that vision God gave him, there is no separation. There will be no more sea. God's people shall be together in a great gathering, one fold in the presence of our one Shepherd.

I am not denying that heaven also is a beautiful city

with domes and spires and foundations of precious stones. It has gates of pearl and streets of transparent gold. But these are just material things in themselves. They could never make heaven. If you were there by yourself, what would it be looking at pearly gates or walking on golden streets? The gathering together of the people is what makes it truly heavenly.

An old minister was speaking to his people and he said, "You know, when I was a little boy and thinking about heaven, I thought of it as a place of golden streets and pearly gates and angels, full of strangers, none of whom I knew. My little brother died, and I began thinking about heaven with the golden streets and pearly gates and angels, filled with strangers but with one little face that I knew. As the years passed my father and mother died." Then more years passed and some of his children died, and then his wife and friends. Then he said, "Now as I stand today, I don't think of heaven anymore as being full of strangers. I think of heaven now as where all of my family has gone, while I tarry behind. Now," he said with tears in his voice, "I know far more who are over there than who are here." That is heaven. It is a gathering of his people, the communion and fellowship of God's saints. Without them it is emptiness and nothingness.

There is a sad story of a seriously ill mother whose daughter was taken away by some friends. They thought it best to keep the little girl until her mother would get well. But in the providence of God tragedy struck and the mother died. After the funeral and after a few days had passed, the friends thought the time had come to bring the little girl back home. She went into her home and called, "Mommie!" And then from room to room, calling out for her mother. Then rushing back to the friends she pleaded, "Where is my mother?" When the friends told her she was gone, the girl burst into tears and sobbed, "Take me away. I don't want to be here without my mother."

We would all feel the same way. We do not want to be here without our loved ones. We want to be with our loved ones, and we will be. And that is heaven. It is the gathering of all God's people.

There shall be one fold and one shepherd.

Heaven Must Be Chosen

Heaven is an election—a selection. Not everyone is going to heaven, and God's Book is very clear on that. Unfailingly heaven is an aristocracy of holiness, humility, confession, and salvation. Heaven is only full of God's elect. Their election can be seen in the choices they make, in what they set their heart on to love. First Corinthians 2:9 says, "Eye hath not seen, ear hath not heard, neither have entered into the heart of man, the things God hath prepared for those who love him." Heaven is a choice of those who love God. Second Timothy 4:8 emphasizes this again. "Henceforth there is laid up for me a crown of righteousness, which the Lord, the righteous judge, shall give me at that day: and not to me only, but unto all them also that love his appearing." God's people earnestly desire the coming of Jesus.

Now frankly, if we did not love God and God's people, we probably would not be happy in heaven. Those not going to heaven really would not be very satisfied there anyway. I could illustrate this with a story I heard once of two excursion boats on either side of a pier in New York Harbor. One of them was a Sunday School class going out for a picnic, and the other was for some bartenders going out for a hullabaloo. There came a fellow running down the pier as fast as he could. He was late. One of those boats had already gone and one of them was still there. But he did not know there were two possibilities. He just saw the boat gradually moving away. Well, he was one of the bartenders, and he was running for all he had because he did not want to miss the party. He leaped over the pier and landed on the deck of that boat as it pulled out and away. And unfortunately he jumped on the "wrong" boat. That bartender was miserable all day, I do not have to tell you, with the Sunday School class. But candidly I would have been miserable on the other boat. Those who "miss the boat" to heaven probably would not have wanted to go anyway. Heaven is a selection. We must choose to love God and God's people.

It is also an election of humility and contrition. "For thus saith the high and lofty One that inhabiteth eternity, whose name is Holy; I dwell in the high and holy place with him also that is of a contrite and humble spirit" (Isa. 57:15). It is a gathering together of those who bow in the presence of the Lord, and who are humble and contrite in their spirit.

I attended the Sunday service of a church at Leningrad, Russia, and I saw many new and surprising things. I had not seen so many tears in a service in all of my life as I saw in that church. It was hard for me to follow what they were saying, but as they knelt and prayed and cried and sang, I just wept, too.

The services there last for hours and hours. In that particular service the pastor began reading letters to the congregation, and as he read they would weep. The more letters he read the more they would weep. I turned to our guide and said, "What are they weeping for? What are those letters?" The guide said to me, "These are letters from members of the church, mostly family, who under the terrible persecution of the Soviet government had left the church and renounced the faith and embraced Communism and given up their Lord. These letters are letters of confession and contrition, wanting to be taken back into the church." As they read those letters the people wept in joy and gladness as they forgave them and embraced them in the circle of the love and fellowship.

That is the *koinonia*, the communion of the saints once again. That just happens to be a very good description of heaven.

Heaven, Purchased with Blood

Third, heaven is redemption, a throng delivered, redeemed, blood-bought. So many of our hymns and songs speak of this:

> Glory, I'm saved! Glory, I'm saved!
> My sins are all pardoned,
> My guilt is all gone.
> I'm saved by the blood of the Crucified One!
>
> —S. J. HENDERSON

Consider Revelation 1: "Unto him who loved us, and washed us from our sins in his own blood . . . to him be glory and dominion forever and ever, Amen" (vv. 5-6). See Revelation 5: "Thou art worthy to take the book, and to open the seals thereof: for thou wast slain, and hast redeemed us to God by thy blood out of every kindred, and tongue, and people and nation" (v. 9). And Revelation 7: "What are these which are arrayed in white robes? . . . These are they which . . . have washed their robes, and made them white in the blood of the Lamb" (vv. 13-14).

Heaven is a redeemed, purchased throng. It is the fruit of our love and tears and prayers. Oh, how true that is! There is not a father or mother alive that does not know the tears and the intercession and hope pressed for their child. We just do. Or even beyond the family circle, the prayers for a loved friend redeemed through our tears of intercession. Heaven is blood-bought.

One of our great evangelists tells how he went back to his farm home where his mother had been ill for twenty years. And he said, "Mother, I sometimes almost lose my faith and fall into doubt when I see you suffer so. I cannot understand it. In the city where I live I know a woman who lives in a stone mansion, and she is affluent and has health, and she has damned more lives than any woman that I know of. And you, Mother, here, for twenty years you have suffered pain, and I don't understand. I can hardly hold onto God." The mother replied, "Son, do you see that old barn there and that old orchard there? Son, there is not ten feet of ground around this house or on this farm where my knees have not been pressed against the ground, praying for you when you were a drunkard and a gambler and thief. In the days when I am most torn in pain and illness, Jesus has been the nearest to me. Had I not been near enough to Jesus for him to hear my voice, you might not have been saved."

The pain of her life made Jesus seem the nearer to her. She was close enough to get his ear when she prayed in behalf of that wayward and prodigal son. The blessed tears of a sainted mother! Virtually all of us will be trophies of grace, because somebody loved us and wept over us and prayed for us.

Oh, the preciousness of our dear Savior and his people!